AMERICAN TRADITIONAL

A COMPREHENSIVE GUIDE TO HOME DECORATING THE ETHAN ALLEN WAY

BY GENEVIEVE FERNANDEZ

SIMON AND SCHUSTER
NEW YORK

To my mother, Alice Fisch,
and Robert L. Ficks, Jr., my valued mentor and friend

Published by Simon and Schuster, A Division of Simon & Schuster, Inc.,
Simon & Schuster Building, Rockefeller Center, 1230 Avenue of the Americas,
New York, New York 10020

SIMON AND SCHUSTER and colophon are registered trademarks of Simon & Schuster, Inc.

Designed by Levavi & Levavi

Manufactured in the United States of America

10 9 8 7 6 5 4 3 2 1

Library of Congress Cataloging in Publication Data

Fernandez, Genevieve.
  American traditional.

  Includes index.
  1. Interior decoration—United States. 2. Deco-
ration and ornament, Early American. I. Ethan Allen,
Inc. II. Title.
NK2003.F4 1984   747.213   84-10548
ISBN: 0-671-47687-4

CONTENTS

INTRODUCTION

This is a book about American Traditional decorating, about a way of "feathering our nests" that is as comfortable and comforting to us today as it was to the colonists, hundreds of years ago, when they first began to create and evolve this uniquely satisfying decorating style.

Traditional decorating is not, of course, exclusively American in origin, nor is it exclusively English either. Much of American Traditional furniture did derive from English prototypes, but the furniture chosen for today's rooms, with the exception of designs that are unmistakably modern, hark back to a diversity of periods and cultures— German Biedermeier, French Empire, Spanish, Oriental, Venetian, and so on. Some of these genres are more popular and more enduring than others; French Provincial, or "country" French, is one example. Other traditional modes come and go, are in or out of favor, depending upon the whims of fashion, which may stress casual, understated furnishings one season and a return to formality the next.

What is interesting, and in a real sense unique, about American Traditional decorating is that its popularity is never affected by the trends of fashion. It continues to proliferate as a much-favored decorating style of the twentieth century, not only here but in other countries as well.

Why should a style of decorating born more than three hundred years ago enjoy this ongoing popularity, and be more viable than ever in today's homes? The reasons are many—some tangible and obvious, others subtle but no less significant.

It is all but impossible to resist the emotional and aesthetic appeal of American Traditional furniture's venerated standards of design: shapes that are remarkably graceful and pretty, scale that is never heavy or overbearing. Traditional

Restored Gardner-Pingree House in Salem, Massachusetts. Adjacent parlors eloquently mix Chippendale, Duncan Phyfe, and Sheraton designs of the period.

furniture is light and beautifully balanced. The gentle patina of mellow woods, the delicately wrought hardware, radiantly colored and patterned Oriental or braided rugs, fabrics woven or printed with Colonial motifs—all appeal to our hearts as well as our eyes. We know that in choosing American Traditional furnishings, we endow our own homes with the same treasured qualities of character and hospitality that fill the pages of books on the decorative arts, or can be seen in the many superb restorations across our land.

What is so comforting about American Traditional furniture is the sense of handwork that not only permeates time-worn and time-honored antiques, but is also expressed in designs that have been manufactured with today's most up-to-date and efficient technology. Wisely and skillfully used, this technology provides not only furnishings of fine value, but a decor that carefully preserves the cherished hallmarks of American Traditional styling. New tables or cabinets come to the marketplace manufactured with the aged patina of a family heirloom. One cannot resist the soul-satisfying pleasure of touching their "nicks," "dents," or "worm-holes." Seating designs emulate the beloved shapes of yester-year, such as serpentine camel backs and the once protective, now purely decorative "wings" on high-back chairs. Yet all these designs are sturdy and sound, built to last for generations.

The enormous emotional appeal of this furniture style is but one reason for its ever-growing and ever-widening popularity. Another is the marvelous adaptability of traditional design structure for the needs of contemporary living. Coffee tables of all shapes and sizes evolved as an alternative to the Colonial tea table. Sofas, which usually require a coffee table, were seldom used in earlier times, when most seating groups were composed of chairs and stools. As space-shy houses required more vertical storage, wall units proliferated in American Traditional styling. Cabinetry has recently been designed to house the most complicated of electronic entertainment equipment. China and curio cabinets are lighted

A keeping room in an American home in Nebraska gains its charm from a collection of magnificent American antiques. (*Colonial Homes* magazine)

from within; dining tables contract or expand with ease to accommodate a few members of the family or a large dinner party.

The American Traditional decorating style has become so broad and diverse in scope and design that it can now be used to express almost any decorative look, and to satisfy the living needs of any specific lifestyle. The choice of furniture designs and their arrangement; the selection of rugs, fabrics, and wallpapers; the application of color; the character of wall hangings and accessories can spell the difference between a home that closely follows the style and mood of a Colonial house and one that irreverently mixes and matches to create a look that is as much a part of today's world as it was of yesterday's.

Use this enduring and timeless decorating style to express your personal taste and living requirements. You may prefer a home that re-creates, unabashedly, the look of an eighteenth-century abode, or you may want a more eclectic style. The choice is yours; the possibilities are endless. It is up to you to take this truly wonderful decorating genre and shape it to your heart's content. This book will help point your way.

FOREWORD

In the four centuries since the crude cabins of the first settlers spelled refuge and security, Americans have had a continuing and creative concern for the environment of their homes. Arriving on our shores with only a few treasured possessions, holding to memories of a distant homeland as they faced the uncertainties of a hostile New World, our forefathers strove to create the ambiance of the homes they had left behind. As they were more and more able to cope with the rigors of a new lifestyle, they began to fashion their own furniture, develop their own colors, weave their own fabrics, and decorate simple furniture and bare walls and floors with paint and pattern.

Wave after wave of colonists and immigrants followed, bringing with them the cultural influences of their native lands, ranging from the superb cabinetry and formal elegance of eighteenth-century England to the sturdy carvings and massive stature of Dutch furniture, the simple, chaste designs of the Spanish, and the ornate, romantic painted styles of German peasant farmers. Houses were built with separate rooms for sleeping, dining, entertaining, and studying. Furnishings became more luxurious, windows larger and window treatments more elaborate; the floors were fitted with custom-made carpets. In their ability to adapt and shape the vestiges of the past to the exigencies of the present, our ancestors set an enduring precedent.

In the ensuing years, America has passed through numerous transient influences in home-furnishing design—Victorian, Oriental, Mission, Art Moderne—popular in their day, and occasionally contributing to a growing American style that is hailed around the world today for its beauty and excellence. The simple, commonsense idea of a wing chair that shuts out a draft . . . the exquisite hallmarks of the great English and American designers and cabinetmakers . . . the simplicity and brilliant engineering for function and utility of the Shakers . . . are among a host of cherished elements that have been blended with today's skills and technology to create home furnishings that retain the best of our past for our homes today.

It is not only for their sense of history and "roots" that American Traditional home furnishings are so highly esteemed. Of perhaps greater importance is their reflection of the solid human values that helped build America to the greatest nation on earth—values that brought the first settlers to this country; values that were instilled at home, passed on from one generation to the next; values that placed the concept of creating "a good home" for one's family above the mere acquisition of fame or wealth. To all of us at Ethan Allen, that's what it's really about.

Since the first piece of Ethan Allen furniture was created in the mid-1930s at our Beecher Falls, Vermont, plant, our special mission and commitment has been to nourish and expand the treasured and decorative heritage of American traditions in home furnishing. Today, Ethan Allen is by far the world's largest and best-known producer of meticulously crafted reproductions and adaptations reflecting the best of American Traditional design.

Nearly 2,000 individual furniture styles are produced by quality-minded craftsmen in 33 facilities throughout the United States, each specializing in a particular product. Other decorative home furnishings and accessories, including lamps, clocks, and Oriental rugs, are manufactured domestically or imported from abroad. The Ethan Allen collection reaches the public through more than 400 unique retail showcases around the world—the Ethan Allen Galleries.

For more than fifty years, Ethan Allen has been committed to helping Americans create beautiful home environments, rich in heritage and tradition. We know that to make a good home takes the love, respect, and understanding of those who share in the endeavor. To that end, this book is respectfully dedicated.

NATHAN S. ANCELL

Chairman, Ethan Allen, Inc.

PART ONE

BASIC CONSIDERATIONS

The extraordinary flexibility of the American Traditional decorating style lies in its own diverse genesis: it was not born within a single generation, nor does it bear the stamp of a rigid decorating discipline or immutable formula.

Early colonists managed to bring over a few beloved pieces of furniture from the homes they had fled in England. Although seeking a refuge in the New World, they held to the kind of furnishings that they had known, and with the establishment of New World craftsmen they could have additional pieces made to fill out their homes. Later, the more affluent colonists, living in Eastern Seaboard cities, imported furniture, fabrics, and rugs from abroad. These furnishings were usually adaptations of elegant and mannered designs that had first been created for the English court and then crafted for the aristocracy. As colonists came over in greater numbers, prospered, and erected handsome and luxurious houses, a demand grew for beautiful furniture. It was then that the great cabinetmakers of such eastern cities as Newport, Philadelphia, and New York emerged, the true forefathers of the American Traditional furniture industry.

It is important to note that while these more elegant and formal designs were being crafted in the cities, homier, rough-hewn, cruder versions were honed by rural carpenters and joiners. Sometimes they used a free imagination to imprint their own aesthetic upon these rustic expressions, and relied upon painted finishes to cover up the woods which were then considered to be of lower quality than the polished mahoganies of the urban designs. So it seems that formal and country interpretations of American Traditional furniture grew up side by side, and ultimately, as we see in many of today's restored houses, lived together under the same roof.

Thus many colonists, in both city and country, began with the few things that had sailed with them across the Atlantic. Over the years they added to this original "trousseau" American-made versions of what was popular in England at the time and, later, other European design heritages as well. This mix of furniture styles was handed down to the next generation, who in turn added designs that became popular and useful during their own life span. As a result, American homes that housed many generations of a single family also collected many generations of American furniture. We see the approach continuing as more and more Americans combine with great ease and facility an American antique with a new reproduction, or interject a bold contemporary element such as a glass-topped table, a complement of straight-lined seating modules, or an explosively colored modern canvas.

Many of us search within our own homes for an affirmation of the gentler and simpler values that seem to be vanishing in this highly technical and computerized world. The graceful lines and rich character of American Traditional furnishings offer a sense of personal identity and a way to soften, with restrained embellishment, stark modern architecture and banal, boxy rooms. For American Traditional is a romantic decorating style that rediscovers the past for the present, a journey into nostalgia that satisfies the modern soul while utilizing today's technology to its own advantage.

Decorating with American Traditional furnishings requires a knowledge of the American design heritage as it has evolved over the centuries. If you want a home that is a close adaptation

CHAPTER 1
THE AMERICAN TRADITIONAL DESIGN HERITAGE

of eighteenth-century Queen Anne interiors, for example, you will need to have as much information as possible about the furniture, fabrics, rugs, and decorative accents that were favored at that time. On the other hand, if you are planning to combine American Traditional with contemporary design for a freer, eclectic, and more personalized effect, you will still want to know the salient features of the predominant style mood with which you are working.

The superb furniture designs from our heritage offer the enduring qualities of comfort, grace, beauty, and adaptability. In tracing the lineage of these designs, we discover that historical categories, while precise in terms of furniture design, shape, materials, and finishes, tend to overlap. The shape of a table leg or chair back that first evolved in an earlier period may still be flourishing at a later time, though perhaps expressed with greater embellishment or ornamentation, or given a more dramatic interpretation. Splat backs on chairs, broken pediments on the tops of cabinets, and cabriole legs used for tables and chairs are examples of designs that were continually reinterpreted from one style period to another.

A bedroom of the 17th-century Buttolph-Williams house in Wethersfield, Connecticut, showing Jacobean and William & Mary furniture.

But while we cannot trace the ancestry of American Traditional furniture as an exact science, we can certainly point out the significant features and changes. Most style periods within the spectrum of American Traditional are identified with a ruling English monarch, or, as in the case of Chippendale or Sheraton, a leading English cabinetmaker of the era.

The time periods in which these style categories dominated the American furniture landscape do not coincide with the years of a monarch's rule or a cabinetmaker's preeminence. It often took many years for a new design concept to cross the Atlantic and take root and flourish in the New World.

The Jacobean furniture brought over by colonists settling in the early seventeenth century seems to have been the first important style genre to emerge in Colonial America. Named after James I, King of England from 1603 to 1625, these rather massive furniture designs were made almost exclusively of oak, as cruder expressions of the court furniture favored at that time. The Pilgrim carvers and joiners who crafted their own versions of Jacobean in this country (from about 1650 to 1690) adopted the large proportions and geo-

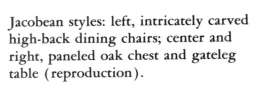
Jacobean styles: left, intricately carved high-back dining chairs; center and right, paneled oak chest and gateleg table (reproduction).

metric carvings reflective of the style's Elizabethan ancestry, but modified them to suit the smaller Colonial houses. Certain features distinguished these large and dark furniture designs, among them melon and rope turnings, bulbous supports and stretchers, carved aprons and foliated scroll carving, paneled doors, low chair rails, wainscot or paneled chairs, and the trestle table, first described as "table board and frame."

The chest was a popular piece of furniture during this early Jacobean period, because it offered ample storage area in Colonial houses that contained no closets, and because its low height allowed it to do double duty as a seating design. Often the chest was the only piece of furniture the early settlers could take with them on their journey over the Atlantic. Craftsmen working in America made these chests of carved and paneled oak, with a plain top instead of the English paneled style, so that it could afford a comfortable seating surface. A miniature version of the storage chest, called the "Bible box," was utilized to store valuable documents, jewelry, and other personal treasures. As the local American carver/carpenter had crude and few tools, limited time, and no fine example of an English design to serve as a

model, he applied split balusters to flat surfaces rather than the more elaborate bas reliefs of the English prototypes.

While Jacobean furniture dominated American homes during the latter half of the seventeenth century, the final decade of that century saw the emergence of a new style named for William of Orange and his wife, Mary, who ascended the English throne as joint rulers in 1689. The William & Mary style differed markedly in some ways from the Jacobean designs from which it evolved. The scale of the furniture was lighter. Furniture was now made of walnut, maple, and other woods, as well as oak; its look was more decorative, and in some instances, more formal. Chests were now supported by a frame fashioned from several of the "inverted cup" or trumpet legs and ball or bun feet. Indented or sinuous reverse cyma curves shaped the stretchers.

Frames were usually low, but soon higher frames were employed to support these chests, marking the beginnings of the beloved highboy in the nomenclature of American design. As the highboy developed, doors on the front of the chests were replaced by drawers.

Tall secretaries, supported by bun feet and featuring large overhanging cornices, also became popular during this period. Even more significant was the development of the table, with a whole new vocabulary of design elements dramatizing the new importance of this furniture category: butterfly tables, more refinement and greater diversity in gateleg tables, tavern tables, and trestle tables.

The gateleg table was often used for dining, as the colonists prospered and could afford to set aside a separate place within their houses to serve as a self-contained dining room. The new prosperity also encouraged the design of more decorative details, such as the crown crest motifs on chair tops, as well as the use of cane for the backs and seats of the first daybeds or chaises longues—essentially banister-back chairs extended by six feet and supported by as many as eight legs.

British trade with the Orient was intensified during the reign of William and Mary, who brought from Holland the Dutch passion for Orientalia. It was at this time that the

William & Mary styles: top, furniture in a new, lighter scale, grouped in a paneled sitting room; center, caning detail distinguishes elegant side chair; bottom, a contemporary adaptation of a high-back love seat.

fine art of japanning, the highly decorative painting of furniture, really emerged. This was indeed a superb way to endow the new furniture styles with color and design impact. Designs were painted on furniture in raised effects over a painted background of black or apricot red. The Guilford chest, made in the Connecticut town of that name, was an outstanding japanned piece of the period, utilizing stylized flowers, leaves, stems, blossoms, and other motifs that were primarily of Dutch inspiration. Other, more formal designs, such as the new highboys, relied upon chinoiserie themes such as camels, pagodas, temples, birds, and Oriental figures. The pendent, or "teardrop," pulls favored for these chests were prettier and more delicate than earlier hardware styles. The japanning techniques were an effective way of transforming pine and maple cabinets into elegant and elaborate designs.

The wing chair entered Colonial houses during this period; its bulbous stretcher and tapered Spanish feet distinguish it from the wing designs of later decades. In New England, the ladder-back chair was developed, a design that was ultimately to become the quintessential American country-style seating design. These early ladder-backs were sometimes made with as many as three to seven rungs or slats, and with a seat of woven rush or rope.

While Queen Anne reigned in England from 1702 to 1714, the style that bears her name did not penetrate American furniture design until about 1720. Queen Anne designs demonstrated a new grace and a restrained elegance that contrasted markedly with the William & Mary designs and the even more massive Jacobean styles that preceded them.

This was the beginning of the golden age of furniture in England and America, a period noted for a proliferation of beautifully designed and crafted furniture that was to have immeasurable significance in the American decorative arts. Heavy legs gave way to the elegant cabriole shape; gracefully curving broken scroll pediment or "bonnet" tops raised the once flat-topped highboys toward the ceiling; and shell ornamentation expressed a new mood in furniture design. The

Queen Anne styles: above, two contemporary expressions of the cabriole leg; above right, shell carving; right, the popular splat-back chair and a pedestal accent table.

exquisitely graceful chairs and tables that emerged at this time were among the most important of Queen Anne contributions. The backs of chairs featured curved stiles and vase-shaped splats, while cabriole legs ended in a ball-and-claw foot. Carved shell motifs enhanced the tops of chair splats, and added rich detail to the knees of chair legs. Other new forms also came into favor at this time, among them the high tea table with pull-out shelves for candles, large drop-leaf tables, candle-stand tables, and beautifully scaled desks. Batwing hardware ornamented the fronts of cabinet drawers, and the upholstered wing chair, with its new cabriole-shaped front legs, displayed a prettier and more elegant profile. So did the Queen Anne corner chairs, a refinement of an earlier design, now utilizing the cabriole legs and vase-shaped splats that were the favored motifs of Queen Anne seating styles.

Thomas Chippendale, the great English cabinetmaker who held sway during the years 1750 to 1785, borrowed the new and refined Queen Anne shapes of his predecessors but expressed them in a far more elaborate and formal manner; the influence of China trade can also be seen most dramatically in these designs, which were to dominate the craft of the Eastern cities in the middle and latter part of the eighteenth century.

Because Colonial cabinetmakers had the use of Chippendale's book *The Gentleman and Cabinet-Maker's Director,* which included more than two hundred illustrations, there was a proliferation of magnificently crafted Chippendale-inspired furniture throughout the Eastern cities. Among those cabinetmakers who were to make their mark in these extraordinary interpretations of Chippendale ideas were William Savery and Benjamin Randolph of Philadelphia; John Townsend and John Goddard of Newport, Rhode Island; Benjamin Frothingham and John Cogswell of Boston; and others who comprised the New York and Baltimore schools.

The new straight, reeded front legs were among the Chippendale innovations that most influenced the profile of American chairs and sofas. Another was the cabriole leg's baroque turn, with elaborately carved ball-and-claw feet.

The plain and solid splats of the Queen Anne chairs were now replaced by pierced splats for a more decorative effect. "Cupid's bow" shaping—a set of three curves in a downward design—gave a new, fancier look to the top rail of chairs, and the shape of the chair back as a whole was rectangular rather than oval. Arms curved dramatically outward, and carved embellishment was employed everywhere—on top rails, pierced splats, cabriole knees, and front stretchers.

New York and Philadelphia cabinetmakers developed the first settees at this time. These were fashioned from two or three chair backs combined to form one seat and then upholstered. The back of the settee had a serpentine curve, and the arms were rolled.

The Chippendale highboy, a rococo version of the simple Queen Anne cabinets that preceded it, was an example of eighteenth-century craftsmanship at its finest. Made of mahogany, it featured elaborately carved scrolls framing a miniature bust or urn at the top. Depending upon the school of cabinetmaking, fretwork or dentil molding ornamented the upper doors and rails, while elaborate carving enriched all door and drawer fronts.

New taller secretaries, blockfront chests, and kneehole desks also flowered during the Chippendale period. The inside compartments of these desks and secretaries were as beautifully detailed and designed as the outside facades. Other important design innovations included the camel-back sofa, a curved-back, straight-legged refinement of the settee. The period was also distinguished by a greater interest in decorative hardware, such as the new batwing designs.

After the American Revolution, the new Federal style, emerging from the design books of Thomas Sheraton and George Hepplewhite and from the neoclassic inspiration of the leading English architect Robert Adam, changed the look of American furniture design.

Satinwood, used with mahogany veneers, was employed by cabinetmakers to evolve desks, tables, and chairs in the new classic mode. Legs of both chairs and tables were more slender and tapered than the earlier styles, and sofas were either curved in the Hepplewhite style or squared off in the Sheraton manner, with tapered and reeded rounded legs.

Heart-shaped shield-back chairs were typical of the Hepplewhite style, and Sheraton designs featured open square backs, often employing vase-and-festoon decoration or reeded, simply pierced banisters. Popular during the early part of the nineteenth century, the most beautiful of the Sheraton designs were desks and secretaries with drawer and door fronts exquisitely ornamented with female figures, medallions, and other classic motifs achieved by means of intri-

Chippendale styles: opposite page, broken-pediment highboy, pierced splat-back and ladder-back chairs, lowboy, and blockfront chest; above, a contemporary interpretation of a Chippendale armchair.

A reproduction of a Chippendale secretary.

cate marquetry and veneering. Such veneering also endowed the newer, larger sideboards, important additions to the more formal dining rooms of this era, with an exceptionally elegant and beautiful presence.

American Empire (roughly 1815–1840) followed closely upon the heels of the Federal style, and was given impetus by the French Empire fashions in furniture design that blossomed under the rule of Napoleon. This period, best exemplified by the work of Duncan Phyfe, also celebrated classic shapes and motifs. New lyre backs on chairs became all the rage, dining tables were now supported by elegant pedestals, and tambour fronts, first noticed in the Federal period, became even more popular for desks and cabinets at this time. Sofas emulated Roman curves, and half-columns were applied to the sides of chests to support the projecting top drawers and to add embellishment.

We should mention here the Windsor chair, a design born in England but evolved in America, independent of prevailing styles, over a period of one hundred and twenty-five years. The Windsor's ancestry can be traced to a peas-

Top left, a shield-back love seat mixes with other delicate Hepplewhite designs; bottom left, high Sheraton serving cabinet for formal dining; above, ornamental classic shapes in American Directoire/Empire living room.

ant's cottage near Windsor Castle, and its American counterpart was first manufactured in this country about 1725. The popularity of this chair spread quickly to the Eastern Seaboard cities and was expressed in a diversity of ways.

Essentially, the Windsor chair was composed of spindles for its back, a solid seat, and turned, splayed legs secured by stretchers. There are many variations on the theme, the best-known including the comb-back, hoop-back, fan-back, and

The ubiquitous Windsor design, here expressed in a settee.

New England arm styles. These Windsors became great favorites of the Colonists because of their distinctively light and airy look and the substantial durability of their hand-wrought construction which securely anchored the spindles and legs. Windsors were made from an assortment of woods: ash or hickory for the spindles, seats of pine or beech, legs from oak or maple. The chairs were often painted to cover up these medleys; favored colors were green, red, yellow, black, brown, gray, and blue. Windsors were made with or without arms, and sometimes as rocking chairs.

Because Queen Victoria's reign was such a long one (1837–1901), it is understandable that more than one specific genre has come to be known as Victorian design. Some of the earliest so-called Victorian styles were borrowed from the Gothic shapes of medieval architecture. Next came a short-lived Elizabethan revival period, and after that the rococo designs associated with John Henry Belter. Heavy and richly ornamented Renaissance Revival designs were popular immediately after the American Civil War. Victorian designs were derivative, for the most part, and Victorian interiors were typically ornate, overdecorated, and cluttered, especially in the later years.

It was not surprising, therefore, that "Reformed" furniture designs emerged in reaction to the elaborate Victorian pieces and heavily decorated interiors. Typical of this backlash were the restrained Gothic shapes of the English architect Charles Locke Eastlake and the simple, straight-lined, purely functional, and honestly crafted Mission furniture of William Morris.

Other nineteenth-century styles that influenced furniture making as a whole include the highly functional and beautifully crafted designs of the Shaker communes, where gratuitous embellishment was considered sinful. Built-in cabinetry began with the Shakers; the handyman's bed, chairs with woven tape seats, household utensils, and marvelously shaped boxes and baskets were other Shaker contributions.

Another important influence upon American nineteenth-century furniture design was the bentwood chair, first designed by Michael Thonet in Vienna. His sons were later to set up shop in New York City, and ultimately their chairs and other seating designs fashioned from frames of bent wood became an important furniture idiom throughout the country.

Those of us who wish to see beautifully restored traditional interiors filled with the finest examples of seventeenth-, eighteenth-, and nineteenth-century American craftsmanship can visit some of the many historical restorations that exist within the United States. Most of these restorations, quite naturally, are located within what had been the original thirteen colonies.

One of the most extraordinary of these restorations is the Henry Francis du Pont Winterthur Museum, which contains some of the finest examples of American architecture and furniture from the years 1640 to 1840. More than two hundred rooms include settings of the William & Mary period, elegant Queen Anne and elaborate Chippendale interiors, classic Sheraton rooms, Hepplewhite and Federal parlors, and also rustic country versions of rooms more common

Ornately framed and tufted seating designs, marble-topped tables, gilt and oversized mirrors, and fanciful window treatment are typical period elements of this large Victorian drawing room.

outside the cities, in small towns and villages. There are also Shaker and Empire interiors; indeed, the museum is a repository of every major design influence on American furniture during the two centuries its collections span.

Other remarkable collections of American period styles are housed within a variety of eighteenth-century restored homes in Colonial Williamsburg, once the capital of Virginia. Furniture designs run the gamut from the formal pieces of the Governor's Palace and the Nicholson house to the provincial or country antiques found in the keeping rooms of smaller homes. And there are many other wonderful restorations throughout Virginia, such as Monticello in Charlottesville, Kenmore in Fredricksburg, Gunston Hall in Lorton, and the Wickham-Valentine house in Richmond. Most of the furnishings within these restorations represent

This simple sitting room reflects the lasting beauty of functional Shaker designs.

PERIOD STYLES OF AMERICAN FURNITURE

PERIOD	GENERAL STYLE	SPECIAL FEATURES & ORNAMENTATIONS	PRINCIPAL FORMS OF FURNITURE
I. Jacobean 1603–1625	Heavy, strong pieces made principally of oak	Turned legs, heavy rounded feet, rounded-arched panels	Large chests; cupboards of every variety; gateleg and trestle tables; stools and benches (more commonly than chairs)
II. William & Mary 1690–1725	Lighter construction; greater height and freedom of design; formal order symmetry	Baroque with richly inlaid surfaces; C-scroll carving and deep turning; serpentined and scroll legs	Daybed; dressing table; high chest or chest on frame; easy chair; high-backed chairs and wing chairs; gateleg table
III. Queen Anne 1725–1760	Quieter, subtler designs with lower proportions, strength with balance, and graceful curves; adapted to scale and comfort of the human body; mahogany and walnut construction	Waving and serpentine lines; ornamentation selectively placed on broad surfaces; S-shaped and cabriole lines; shell carving and tall spoon backs	Upholstered easy chairs; high tea table with pull-out shelves
IV. Chippendale 1750–1780	Greater freedom of movement in designs, overall instability of composition; use of lush figured silks and damasks, polished leather, elegant crystal, ruffles, and lace	Higher and more spirited carved ornamentation; S-shaped scrolls evolved into swirls; brilliantly carved and figured surfaces	Fretted and galleried tea tables; stands for china jars; girandoles; bureau tables and large-scale library furniture; fire screens; settees and high-boys with ball-and-claw feet
V. Federal 1780–1810	Neoclassical visions of lightly poised and correct taste; both curvilinear (Hepplewhite) and rectilinear (Sheraton) silhouettes; practical yet delicate; lightly ornamented	American eagle emblem—patched, etched, hammered, or cast	Secretaries and desks with slender legs; worktables, basin stands, night tables; sideboards with closed cupboards and drawers

VI. American Empire 1820–1840	Exemplified by Duncan Phyfe; tapered reeding on turned legs; reeding and fluting on chair, sofa, and table legs	Lyre as classical decorative motif; cast brass animal-paw feet and brass casters	Dining tables with elegant pedestals, tambour fronts
VII. Victorian 1840–1900	Contrast of hard, powerful, massive objects with small, soft, and delicate objects; Gothic details and curving rococo elements fused with ancient classical forms	Natural images of birds, fruit, leaves, and vines; ornamented fabrics	Gadget furniture; reclining chairs and lounge beds
VIII. Reform 1870	Reaction to factory-made furniture and overfrilled ornamentation exemplified by Mission furniture of William Morris; angular and sleeker forms	Crisp, firm upholstery; planes replacing curves; return to traditional oak joinery	The Morris chair

middle- and late-eighteenth-century and early-nineteenth-century designs.

Another state rich in restorations is Maryland, with its Myrtle Grove near Easton, Ratcliffe Manor in Talbot County, the Harwood-Hammond house in Annapolis, Widehall in Chestertown, and many other fine period homes.

There are also superb restorations worth seeing in the New England states. The Gardner Pingree House, the Pierce Nichols House, and the Crowninshield-Bentley house are all extraordinary restorations in Salem, Massachusetts. Among others worth visiting in Massachusetts is Hancock Shaker Village, with its superb collection of Shaker furnishings and household designs.

Some of the best-known restorations in New York State include Van Cortlandt Manor at Croton-on-Hudson, Phillipsburg Manor at Tarrytown, and Boscobel, with its exquisite Adam interiors, at Garrison-on-Hudson.

The entire spectrum of restorations are too numerous to mention here.* Some of the more outstanding are the houses at Wethersfield, Connecticut; Andulusia in New Hope, Pennsylvania; the Gauche House in New Orleans; Monteigne in Natchez, Mississippi; the Spite House in Rockport, Maine; the Three Bricks in Nantucket, Massachusetts; the Gibbes House in Charleston, South Carolina; the Lindens in Washington, D.C.; and Wilton near Richmond, Virginia.

Visiting these superb repositories of American period designs has become a popular American pastime, as families plan a special weekend or even a vacation around a visit to one or more restorations and museums. Before planning such a trip, however, it is important to check on the hours when the restoration is open to the public. Some houses are not available for public viewing, or they may be temporarily closed down for repair or (in houses that are unheated) for the winter season.

Frequenting antiques shops that specialize in American designs and attending auctions of American furnishings will also broaden your understanding of the genre. It's helpful to purchase a catalog that describes each item in such an auction; all furnishings to be sold are usually on exhibit several days before the event.

Sometimes it is hard to decide just how pure and museum-perfect you want your home to be. It's one thing to fall in love with the antique rooms of famous American restorations, but it is quite another to live with a rigidly eighteenth-century ambiance. You may find it helpful to collect magazine photographs of rooms furnished primarily with

* For a complete review of American historic restoration, the reader may refer to *The Golden Treasury of Early American Houses* by Richard Pratt, *100 Most Beautiful Rooms in America* by Helen Comstock, and *The Antiques Book of American Interiors*.

American Traditional designs. After reviewing these clippings on your own or with your family, you can select those interiors that especially appeal to you and that meet the requirements of your lifestyle. In doing this you will discover the way *you* want to handle American Traditional—whether as a purist, or modifying with fresh colors and patterns, or radically updating with modern elements.

Once you start looking for it, you will find American Traditional decoration all around you—including all the finest furniture and department stores. And as you proceed into this book, you will be surprised by the extraordinary variety of ways in which it can be expressed.

The most beautifully decorated home can be a travesty if it does not provide comfort, enjoyment, and ease of use to the family it houses. The requirements of members of your family should in fact

CHAPTER 2
FOR THE WAY YOU LIVE TODAY

be integrated into the design plan of your home, so that each room "works" in the scheme of day-to-day living. This is especially crucial today, when space is itself so expensive that few of us have the luxury of decorating an area purely to fulfill an aesthetic ideal.

It is unlikely, then, that any family living in the 1980s can really want to create for themselves an exact replica of an eighteenth-century home. We are in an age when many women go to work, rather than staying at home baking bread or doing needlework. Today's living room may be the space that contains the most up-to-date electronic entertainment equipment, rather than a parlor where neighbors call for Sunday tea. The exigencies of our faster-paced and more complicated lifestyles require furnishings that are not only durable, but easy to care for. Many rooms have to serve more than one purpose: dining rooms double as family centers; living areas sometimes contain hidden sleeping facilities; bedrooms must often play a round-the-clock role.

The beauty of the American Traditional decorating style is that it adapts so readily to a diversity of living arrangements without losing its character. A home can maintain its ingratiating American flavor, yet also provide a meaningful and colorful abode to all who live within it. The critical

A formal living room with paneled walls, Oriental rug, 18th-century reproductions, and antique accessories for an elegant lifestyle.

challenge of interior design is to discover what those living needs are and to meet them, whether the chosen style be American Traditional, French Provincial, or minimalist modern. Any design approach can be manipulated to serve living priorities, but the process requires more than gut instinct. A certain amount of research and a great deal of planning must be undertaken for one's home to become a true expression of both the tastes and the living needs of the entire family.

Before discovering these important preferences and translating them into a viable home for your family, certain basic decorating principles should be considered.

First, don't feel that you must follow established decorating dogma to the letter. There are always helpful and practical guidelines that can be, and often should be, observed, but within these parameters there is room for self-expression and flexibility, so that the ultimate choices will be your own and your home, therefore, will be a uniquely personal one.

Secondly, unless you are trying to re-create a room from a history book, there is no perfect, no absolutely "right" way to decorate an interior. Often there are several equally good ideas for the same room, and this includes not only design and color choice but also furniture selection and placement. While an understanding of the basics will help you avoid the pitfalls, try not to aim for the most "perfect solution," since this kind of thinking will limit your self-expression, waste a lot of time, and make the task more onerous than enjoyable. Rather than search for the impossible (and the unnecessary), try to express your own and your family's feelings about color and design in relation to the kind of home you live in, the size and shape of your rooms, and the purposes to which they will be put.

You may want to interpret American Traditional in a very fresh and contemporary manner. This is fine, if you do it in a sensible way, rather than trying to apply the latest color fashions, or utilize the trendiest pattern and furniture-arrangement ideas. Decorate your home so that it has staying power, or more exactly, "living power"—the capacity to

BEFORE YOU BEGIN, TAKE INVENTORY

- analyze your lifestyle; try to determine what you are trying to accomplish

- are you single, married with children?

- do you live in a house or an apartment?

- is your home temporary or permanent?

- are you relocating from a small apartment to a much larger one?

- are you moving from a house to an apartment, or an apartment to a house?

- do you entertain often? throw large dinners or small, intimate parties?

last many years longer than a current fad. Decorate your home to please yourself, rather than to impress your friends. Always bear in mind that while trends come and go, good taste as you express it never goes out of style. Creating a contemporary American Traditional home that is comfortable and pretty, rather than dazzling and of the moment, will give it a certain built-in flexibility. At some point in the future you can change it, freshen it, update it, using the same big-investment furnishings that you started with at the beginning.

Remember, above all else, that decorating is *fun.* It can be very rewarding and fulfilling to watch a beautiful home take shape and grow to completion while it functions effectively for yourself and your family.

So, how do you go about creating an environment that you'll enjoy on an ongoing basis? The first step must be to analyze your lifestyle and that of your family in relation to the home in which you live or intend to live. All the decorating principles ever evolved by the experts won't be of any help unless you have a clear understanding of what you are trying to accomplish.

Because your lifestyle is most likely not as dramatic or as clearly defined as that, say, of a film star or jet-setting celebrity, you may think that you don't even have one. But a bit of detective work will prove that you and your family have already developed a way of life with its own characteristics, routines, and activities. To help you discover what these are, here are some examples you may recognize.

Spontaneous party-givers like to entertain in their homes, and how they do it says a lot about their lifestyle. People who throw last-minute get-togethers usually favor informality and casual dining, such as serve-yourself buffet suppers, or simply handled, no-work cocktail parties. A family room complete with its own dining area, or an apartment living-dining room designed for a free flow of traffic is a fine arrangement for this kind of entertaining.

Others, especially professional people who entertain often

Living on a farm with comfort,
color, and country furnishings.

for business reasons, may prefer to have small and relatively stately sit-down dinners in elegant surroundings. So they would want a formal dining room to serve this purpose. And if they give large, beautifully catered parties, they would probably want their living room and dining room to serve as one large entertainment unit.

Parents of young children usually have a lifestyle shaped by their little ones. A storage place for toys and durable furniture are among the top priorities in such a home. Interiors with a young and easygoing style would be appropriate.

Craft- and hobby-oriented people always need work space, good light, and a storage place for materials and equipment. It can be very frustrating to have to stop in the middle of a project and put everything away so that the table can be used for dinner, or to spend hours searching for various paraphernalia stored in assorted closets and cabinets. If you plan your home to accommodate your special hobby in one specific place, you won't have these problems.

Students, too, have pursuits that require space and privacy. A place to read and work, plus a spot to watch television or listen to music, can be important. A corner in the bedroom or a part of the family room or den that can be used exclusively as a study would be an important consideration for a family with school-age children.

Those who work all day may use their homes mainly at night, and their decorating approach should be chosen accordingly. Here, the bright and sunny colors or paler hues might be in order. And for those who have little time to maintain their homes, soil-resistant fabrics, well-organized storage, and a minimum of dust-collecting accessories would also be desirable.

The free-lance professional who works at home, like the hobbyist or student, needs a special and private place to work, but in this instance it would have to be a separate room that could be transformed into a real home office, complete with desk, storage files, and bookshelves.

A working mother will want to spend as much time with her family as she can when she gets home. Very possibly, her house has an open dining-kitchen arrangement, so that she can proceed with food preparation within sight and sound of her family. If not, then the dining area should contain an ample buffet or server. Dinner can be placed here before the meal, so that the lady of the house can spend most of the dinner hour with her family, instead of running back and forth to the kitchen. Low maintenance and soil-resistant materials and furnishings would also be a top requirement.

Other living styles come to mind. An obsessive collector of accessories or folk art, for example, will need ample shelf space to store and display acquisitions. On the other hand, if you prefer a clean, uncluttered, open, and space-expanding look in your home, you will probably keep accents and collectibles to a minimum, or require extensive storage furniture to keep possessions organized and out of the way. If your family really lives in every room of the house, the inevitable spread of books, periodicals, sports equipment, and electronic components will give your home a pleasant sense of clutter, though this should be a controlled disarray, never a chaotic mess, and requires furniture that takes it into account.

The specific lifestyles described above should give you some idea of the kinds of priorities that must be catered to if a decorating plan is to succeed. If you live alone, the process is obviously much simpler, as you need satisfy only your own design and living preferences, following the slightest whim if that whim is important to you. Still, even those who live alone and love their solitude will entertain occasionally, and even put up an overnight guest. Such needs, although perhaps limited, should also be worked into the decorating plan.

If you are married, you must of course consider the needs, tastes, and activities of your spouse. Even if the other expresses little interest in the planning process and plays only a minor role in its execution, he or she will probably have strong feelings about the results. It's important, therefore, that you persuade your mate to participate in making the final decisions.

If you have children, their ages and specific needs will ob-

Rough-hewn woods and a counter-point of textures furnish the living/craft room of a remodeled barn.

46

viously affect the way you decorate their rooms and your house as a whole. With small children, safety is a priority throughout the house. Children's bedrooms should contain furnishings that store their toys and games, perhaps arranged so that there is some floor space for them to play in. There might also be room for a table and set of chairs scaled for a toddler or small child.

A child's age will also help to determine the choice of wall coverings, carpeting, and other textures throughout the house. Scrubbable wall coverings, fabrics treated to soil-resistant finishes, and the avoidance of pale, "fragile" colors make sense in a house filled with rambunctious small fry (as does the stability of smaller pieces of furniture). Older children will not be as hard on these furnishings, but with teenagers in the house you may want to decorate your family room to serve also as a comfortable hangout for them and their friends. Again, durable materials would be a consideration. And of course a household with pets also requires fabrics and colors that stand up to wear and tear.

Where you live will provide additional guidelines to help you draw up your design plan and select furnishings for your home. If you live in a city apartment, you must allow for the special problems of city living, such as the quick accumulation of dirt, dust, and grime. Apartments often have limited closet space, so providing ample storage facilities via cabinets and dressers will be an important consideration. Limited natural light, and the boxy, architecturally sterile rooms typical of new high-rise apartments will also affect the colors you choose and the way you plan your decoration.

Noise also presents a challenge to city dwellers, whether it is the din of street traffic from below or the sounds emanating through thin apartment walls. A good solution is to use wall coverings and carpets that insulate against sound, worked into the design scheme.

A house in the suburbs or country will not have the problem of city dirt or soot, nor will you have to worry about the noise your neighbor's stereo is making (or your own); but here the interplay of indoor-outdoor living presents its own unique problems. Your floors will be much more vulnerable to soil, mud, and snow tracked in from outside. And you will want to relate the decor to the outdoor views, especially if your home has ample window areas.

Vacation or weekend houses pose a special challenge. A house near the beach requires fabrics and floor coverings that stand up to salt air, humidity, and the inevitable sand; and for any house in a warm climate, you will want to choose colors to make it seem as airy and cool as possible. A ski house or country home used often on winter weekends requires a totally different approach. Here colors and textures can help evoke a warm and cozy feeling. Weekend guests are often a fact of life in any kind of vacation house, whether at the beach or in ski country, so extra sleeping facilities provided by dual sleep furniture or built-in bunk beds should probably be on your list of priorities.

Whether you rent or own your home will also affect the way you decorate it, in terms of both the amount of money you spend on it and the kind of investment you make in built-in as opposed to free-standing furniture.

Renters are often restricted in the type of construction they may install or wall coverings they may use, and are usually required to fill in any holes in the walls created by picture hooks or supports for bookshelves, hanging cabinets, and so on. It is important to be aware of these limitations, as well as any other special circumstances, such as the frequency with which the landlord will paint your apartment, if that is indeed his responsibility, and the colors available to you. This question of who does the painting (or wall covering) will undoubtedly shape the overall choice of a color scheme, and may even persuade you to alter or to totally change what you first decided upon and planned your interiors around.

Then, too, if you consider yourself only a temporary resident of your apartment or rented house, you will be more likely to invest in furnishings that will travel with you, rather than install expensive built-ins that have to be left behind. This would apply not only to cabinets and shelving, but also to wall-to-wall carpeting. If you expect to move within a relatively short period, you should buy furniture flexible enough to suit another layout, and possibly to work into a totally different kind of arrangement. This kind of future, alternative planning will be discussed in greater detail in our chapter on furniture choice and arrangement, but it is important to be aware of these considerations at this early stage of your decorating project.

The size and scope of your decorating plan will also depend upon the extent to which your present home is already decorated. When starting completely from scratch, you will have "carte blanche" in all categories and be able to choose new furniture, fabrics, floor coverings, and lamps and other accessories. On the other hand, if you are simply redecorating or refreshing your home with a change of wall colors, new fabrics and window treatments, and possibly new floor coverings, you will be more restricted. Even so, you should still give time and thought to making selections that will transform your home into a more comfortable and usable place for your family, not just a newer-looking and cosmetically prettier one.

You may be planning to move from a small apartment into a much larger one, or may finally have purchased that house of your dreams after years in a cramped tract house. In this instance, you already own a nucleus of furnishings. The challenge here is to successfully integrate your present furnishings with new purchases, so that the finished result is a harmonious living arrangement rather than a hit-and-miss hodgepodge of new and old. Assess the role each room of the new house must play and decide upon the ultimate destiny of each piece of furniture that you plan to take with you. This kind of preplanning may suggest that you sell a cabinet, table, or sofa that simply will not work with your new plan, rather than try to force any of these into the scheme and end up with a compromise that is less than pleasing—and proves penny-wise but pound-foolish.

An even more difficult decorating project is one that calls

for cutting back or retrenching—the effort that must be made when one moves from a larger home to more modest quarters. When children grow up and leave home, parents may decide that they want a maintenance-free condominium instead of their rambling Georgian house. This will also be the case when a newly single parent needs to decorate a new but much smaller home for herself (or himself) and the children.

A move of this nature is especially difficult because it involves paring down—eliminating furnishings to which you may be emotionally attached or which you feel you cannot live without. In such instances you must exert self-discipline and cut the cord that ties you to possessions that have no place in your new home, that if taken with you might not only crowd your rooms but prevent them from expressing the kind of fresh start that you want for yourself. Developing a viable furniture plan and decorating scheme for your new home will give you a working blueprint that will help you evaluate your possessions and figure out what must be eliminated and what can be retained. Keep your favorite paintings and tabletop accessories, but exercise a stern and critical eye toward the furniture you presently own. A certain amount of flexibility in your approach to furniture choices may allow you to keep more of these beloved pieces simply by assigning new roles to them. A favorite desk, for example, could serve as a nightstand in the new bedroom, even if there is no place for it in the living room. A large armoire or broken-pediment highboy, which may have been the star attraction of your old and much larger master bedroom, could occupy some available wall space in your new living room.

Eliminating labels that limit each piece to a living room, bedroom, or dining room can help you salvage favorite possessions when it is necessary to cut back and pare down. So many pieces can be used in other rooms of the house that by evaluating your furniture according to its potential use, rather than as designed for a specific room and specific place, you will discover ways to fit these pieces smoothly and effec-

A commitment to restoration and authentic design prompted the reclamation and furnishing of this 18th-century brick house in Baltimore.

tively into your new home and lifestyle. Changing the roles of your furniture will make them seem like new additions rather than old standbys. This kind of creative approach to furniture choice will undoubtedly make your home more interesting, and more personal as well.

Once you have worked out the most desirable decorating scheme for your new and smaller residence, it will become immediately clear to you which designs are simply no longer feasible. By selling off the surplus pieces, you will accumulate enough money to cover the cost of some of the furnishings really needed to make your new home work best. You will discover that by trading in your large sectionals for a slimmer and shorter sofa, or some decorative cabinets for commodious but compact wall units, you will have stretched the space of your smaller home without having overstretched your budget.

Now that you have come to terms with the logistics of your family's lifestyle, the kind of home you want, and the extent to which you will need to decorate or redecorate, you are ready to assess the tastes and design preferences of your family, and to utilize these considerations in making the necessary choices. How do you acquire this information? Here you must urge your spouse and children (if they are old enough and interested enough) to sit down with you and bounce around some design and color ideas. Now is the time to start collecting a portfolio for each room that you will be decorating. You can assemble such portfolios by continually clipping from home-decorating magazines those photographs of houses, interiors, and color schemes which interest you or appeal to you for one reason or another. Show these to your family and see what they have to say, or what other thoughts the clippings might spark.

If you have collected photographs of a wide range of design moods—from primitive farmhouse Early American to more formal Chippendale or Queen Anne—you will be offering your family a greater choice from which they should have little difficulty zeroing in on the kind of home you all really want—whether a formal one, a relaxed country place, or any of the many mixed styles between these extremes. There is no reason, for instance, why the living and dining rooms cannot be more formal than the family room or bedrooms; indeed, you can vary your expression of American Traditional throughout the house.

The degree of formality or informality you choose for each room will affect not only the choice of furniture, but also the kinds and textures of fabrics and floor coverings you will purchase. If your research has been thorough, you have discovered that it is often the fabric textures and pattern that emphasize or modify the formal nature of the furniture, and you might then decide to look for fabrics that can provide the refinement of mood you desire. A Chippendale wing chair will be just as handsome in a linen print as in a silken brocade, but the choice of fabric will soften or heighten the chair's basic look. By the same token, covering a floor with the more country-style rag rugs or braided designs will achieve a far more informal mood than a grander Oriental, or a rug with a patterned or carved border motif.

Fabrics can also be employed to establish the degree of authenticity of period mood. If you prefer a more contemporized effect, you should choose textures and patterns that are not specifically American Traditional. On the other hand, to reproduce a home with a dramatic eighteenth-century flavor, you would use fabrics that are period-inspired.

You will probably have noticed that those American Traditional rooms which seem more personal and individualized often mix a variety of wood finishes with painted ones, or combine modern upholstery, such as a Parsons-style sofa or contemporary seating modules, with farmhouse tables, hutches, and chests.

Your portfolio should contain color ideas or themes that have stopped your eye as you leafed through magazines and books, even if the room you were clipping did not contain the style of furniture you intend to use. By collecting these color ideas, you will be able to give your family a substantial choice, and you will also have gone through the process of discovering for yourself what color combinations appeal to you most. (The whole subject of color is treated in the next chapter.)

In assembling these "portfolios of possibilities," don't limit yourself to decorating ideas you can afford. Almost any decorating approach can be adapted in a much less costly way.

Also be sure to collect photographs with wall treatments or window ideas that might work in one or several of the rooms you will be decorating. This applies as well to furniture selection and arrangement; often a photograph in a magazine will present an interior that accommodates a floor plan similar to your own, or suggests a fascinating solution that might not have occurred to you otherwise.

You and your family will become more aware of what constitutes good taste as you become more familiar with what professional designers achieve and with what exists in the marketplace. See the model rooms in furniture and department stores, and investigate the quality and cost of what is available. You will automatically be going through the process of selecting and rejecting so necessary to the development of a workable, cohesive decorating plan.

Whatever the styles of that plan, you should be able to furnish your home sensibly and within your budget. Only a few of us can afford the genuine American antiques that are now so rare and costly, but thanks to the ever-growing popularity of the American Traditional style, there is a wealth of beautifully made and superbly adapted reproductions manufactured by firms who specialize in furniture, wall coverings, fabrics, and lamps and other accessories. These are offered in a wide range of prices, and will often incorporate such contemporary concepts as electronic storage, home office facilities, modular storage or seating. In most instances these designs are scaled to fit today's living needs and architectural limitations.

Once you have done all the necessary homework, reviewed your selections with your spouse or family, and pared down your choices, you will notice that certain strong preferences have materialized in terms of color, pattern, and style. You and your family will also have observed from the photographs you've collected that the most pleasing and best-designed interiors display a furniture and color strategy with balance and grace, and that a room filled with exquisite furnishings does not really work if the individual elements do not synthesize into an harmonious whole. In the marketplace you will have observed that some furnishings have a quality look, whereas others seem poorly crafted or not substantial. This does not mean that you have to invest in very expensive furnishings to make certain of quality workmanship, design, and materials. But neither should you try to skimp. The emphasis must be on value, not on price.

The initial stages of a decorating project ought to be slow and painstaking. A home should never be built in a day. The more care and thought you put into the early planning and decisions, the more likely you will be to create the useful, attractive, and meaningful home you and your family will really love and be happy with for a long time. It is only by careful evaluation of the house or apartment you live in, and of the lifestyle and design preferences of the family within it, that you can achieve a successful result. Take your time, modify and change as you go through this process, and be sure to review together the final, fully evolved design approach. And even this final plan may change as you go through the various stages of shopping for your furnishings. Fresh ideas and inspirations may present themselves to you in the form of a new furniture collection, or a fabulous hutch you managed to acquire at a country auction.

Decorating a home is a dynamic process. Within a disciplined structure, there is always room for changes and modifications.

Color is the most readily available and least costly decorating tool we have, but it has not always been so. Certainly it wasn't in those early years when the first settlers built their crude and simple homes. Before the advent of

CHAPTER 3
COLOR

industrial technology, the colonists had to satisfy their desire for color by using the fresh greens of plants and trees, the lively hues of wildflowers, or the more subdued palette of the natural materials of which they built their houses—brick, stone, and wood.

Later colonists were able to develop formulae for squeezing colors out of nature and transforming their walls, floors, fabrics, and furniture into brighter decorative elements. They extracted homemade dyes by brewing colors out of roots, flowers, mosses, and plants to create the greens, browns, blacks, blues, reds, yellows, purples, and oranges we associate with American Traditional color schemes. On occasion, the colonists would add sour milk to one of their home-brewed colors to lighten it.

By the middle of the eighteenth century, oil paints became available for the more affluent colonists, and a wider range of color nuances was possible for walls, woodwork, and exteriors. Softer hues became especially popular at this time, influenced to a large degree by the prevailing color trends in France and England—soft ivories, gray-greens, rose, blue, and yellow. During the Federal period, even paler tones such as light salmon, soft yellow-green, muted red, and a range of pastels came into favor. Then, during the Victorian era, dark reds, browns, greens, and golds dominated the palette of American interiors.

Bold primary colors of red and yellow combine with clear whites in counterpoint with mellow natural tones of brick fireplace and wood beams.

Butolph-Williams House, Wethersfield, Conn.

Those who wish to confine themselves to museum-perfect color selection need only go to their local paint store, where they will find paint "collections" that have been inspired by such great American restorations as Colonial Williamsburg. A perusal of illustrations in reference books on American Traditional decorating will immediately tell you what colors "went" with each period, and you can use this as a guideline to achieve a more authentic effect.

Most Americans, however, choose colors that suit their own tastes and preferences, rather than those of a strict period discipline, and a full understanding of color as a powerful decorating tool becomes necessary. For color can be used to expand or contract space, to camouflage awkward architectural or structural defects, to minimize bulky furniture. We may use color to make our rooms more comfortable, to lift our spirits and soothe our anxieties. Modern technology puts every color of the rainbow at our disposal, both in natural materials and in new synthetics that boast extraordinary clarity of hue. The challenge of using color is to choose from so seemingly limitless a palette those shades, hues, and tints that work best with our furnishings, tastes, and lifestyles.

Color is probably the most powerful ingredient in the decorating plan. Literally, it sets the tone or temperament of the environment; it arrests the eye. When you enter a room, color is the first quality you notice, even before you become aware of shape and design.

Color also has chameleonlike qualities, as it changes tone depending upon the texture in which it is expressed, the other colors with which it is partnered, and the degree to which it is used. No one color is ever new, but there are always new, fashionable, and trendy ways to use color. Color fads, however, should never be adopted unless they promise to wear well, to be suitable and comfortable. Bold, offbeat-colored furnishings cannot be replaced as easily as can the high-fashion dress that may look dated next season. Following fads is always dangerous, and nowhere more so than in the realm of color. A color trend that may stop the eye and

The counterpoint of blue with melon, clarified by white, provides an analogous color scheme.

Blue and white, a favorite combination, lively and serene. The theme works strikingly in this small living room with ample views of the outdoors.

excite the senses for the moment can easily become tiresome before long. Color's power should be exploited to make the home as warm, as interesting, and as pretty as possible, but always in a sensible way.

Color is integral to every decorating project. Major furniture purchases can be postponed, accessories can be added later, but the color plan must be established from the start. Color cannot be an afterthought; its choices and applications will have enormous impact on your floor plan, the design of window treatments, your major and minor purchases.

Of course, color can also be used to renew existing interiors. A new sofa print, a fresh coat of paint on a faded hutch, or bold new linens in a lackluster bedroom might be all that is needed to inject new life into tired rooms.

A room can be vibrant, dramatic, and comforting, or dull, dreary, and dismal simply because of the presence or absence of color. Color does not merely decorate; it affects our emotions. We even use color to articulate feeling: "white with rage," "in a blue mood," "green with envy," "red with shame." Color is an active rather than passive factor, and its energy should be harnessed advantageously in the design of our homes.

Color can make a room seem more formal or more relaxed. It can hype a mood of sparkle and titillation, as in a dining room, or bring quiet and repose to a study or library. Color can dramatize beautiful architectural features such as a fireplace, wainscoting, and molding, and it can synthesize a collection of eclectic furnishings. Whatever its application, color can express a special private vision.

What is color? The basic definition of color is that it is the quality of light reflected to the eye. Light that is not absorbed is seen as color. When a sofa appears to be red, it's because all other colors in a ray of light are absorbed by the sofa except the red rays. A surface appears to be white when all rays of light are reflected, and black when no rays are reflected. Therefore, white is the presence of all colors, and black is the absence of color. (Have you ever noticed that

THE LANGUAGE OF COLOR

HUE: "Color" and "hue" are often used interchangeably to mean the color sensation by which you distinguish the various colors of the spectrum, including the twelve major colors and the many further blendings that produce complex colors.

SATURATION refers to the degree of hue in a color, ranging from a concentration of color to subtle varieties. Red, for example, is the hue that is most distinguishable in the color red. Pink is less saturated with red (and diluted with white).

CHROMA AND INTENSITY are often used to describe the amount of saturation of the color. Intense colors, such as the bright green of early spring grass, are said to be saturated, while sagebrush and avocado are less intense.

PURITY refers to the unadulterated saturation of a color or hue. Whenever a color is blended with another color or neutral, it is less intense than in its pure form or intensity.

colors seem to fade and disappear at nightfall? This is one reason why people who live in dark apartments or who are seldom home can use vibrant colors and strong contrasts in their rooms.)

In pigment, however, as opposed to light, white is the absence of color and black is all colors mixed together. (Actually, white and black are not usually considered color, and in fact, they can both be used in almost any decorating scheme for accent purposes.)

To use color in decorating, you must understand the color system as created by pigments, paints, and dyes. This can best be explained by a simple color wheel showing the three primary colors and those derived from them. It is essential that you understand this wheel; it explains how colors evolve, how they work together, and what special properties are unique to each color in the spectrum. As mentioned earlier, the same color will "read" very differently when paired or teamed with different colors. The proportion or amount of a color used will also alter its appearance, making it seem brighter, bolder, or more restrained.

THE COLOR SPECTRUM

THE PRIMARY COLORS are yellow, red, and blue; they are considered the basic colors, in that they are not created by a mixing of other colors. These three primaries plus three secondary colors, six tertiary colors, and twelve quaternary colors make up the twenty-four colors that compose the wheel.

THE SECONDARY COLORS are created by the mixing of the primaries: yellow and red make orange, red and blue make violet, and blue and yellow blend into green.

THE TERTIARY, OR THIRD-ORDER, COLORS evolve from the mixing of secondaries and adjacent primary colors. For example: yellow and orange become yellow-orange, red and violet form red-violet, orange and red make red-orange, and so on.

(*continued on page 66*)

DECORATE WITH COLOR

- to expand or contract space

- to camouflage awkward architectural or structural details

- to minimize bulky furnishings

- to brighten or lighten a room exposed to very little natural light

- to create warmth or intimacy

- to set the tone of the environment

- to renew existing interiors

- to make a room seem formal or relaxed

THE QUATERNARY, OR FOURTH-ORDER, COLORS are made by the mixing of tertiaries and primaries. Yellow mixed with yellow-orange becomes yellow-yellow-orange. This pattern is followed completely around the wheel.

Colors have three basic properties: hue, value, and chroma. These are used to describe a color's identity, lightness or darkness, and intensity. Each is important in the proper use of color, and each can be varied to achieve certain effects. *Hue* is a color's identity; *value* is the lightness or darkness of a color on a scale from white to black; the *chroma,* or chromatic intensity, of a color is its vividness. Pure, unmixed colors are of the highest chromatic intensity. This intensity can be reduced by the addition of its complement—the color opposite it on the color wheel. The result is not necessarily lighter or darker, but a color that takes on a soft or grayed cast, which makes it less intense. Equal amounts of any two complements mixed together will produce gray. The complement of red is green; the complement of yellow is violet; the complement of blue is orange. In other words, the complement of each primary is the secondary color opposite it on the wheel. Knowing the complements is extremely useful in developing your color schemes.

As we explore the rudiments of color and become acquainted with the color wheel, we can begin to determine how to employ these colors within our homes. Do we simply select two or more harmonious colors from the wheel and apply them willy-nilly? Canary yellow and violet are complementary colors, but we would hardly want to combine them for wall tones. We must first appreciate the special qualities of each of the important color families in order to combine colors intelligently.

The three primary colors—red, yellow, and blue—and the three secondary colors—orange, green, and violet—establish the six most important color categories. Each one offers unique characteristics, both in its pure state and in mixed variations, that can be utilized in formulating the color scheme and integrating that scheme to the design plan.

Color can cool a room, as in this tropical bedroom splashed with white and laced with brilliant accents of lemon, sapphire, and melon.

Exuberant color lightens and brightens a bedroom filled with the wood tones of furniture, paneled walls, and beams.

DESIGNING WITH COLOR

COLOR	DESIGN IMPACT	EFFECTS IN COMBINATION WITH OTHER COLORS
RED	Bold, brave, regal, and sumptuous	w/ neutrals and browns: softer w/ white and gold: more intense w/ yellow: more lively
YELLOW	Lively and cheerful or saucy	w/ white: more radiant w/ black: more substantial w/ red: more boisterous
BLUE	Dependable, versatile, serene, and soothing	w/ white: crisp and versatile w/ yellow: happier w/ red and white together: strong and patriotic w/ coral, peach, and pink: delightfully sophisticated
ORANGE	Scintillating and spicy	w/ neutrals: mellower w/ brown and black: more pungent w/ green: added freshness w/ blue: tempered and tame
GREEN	Powerfully exhilarating but also soothing	w/ yellow and orange: warmer and more brilliant w/ blue: cooler and more elegant w/ white: heightened radiance
PURPLE (VIOLET)	Strong and regal. Similar to red	w/ brown and black: tempered w/ green: elegant w/ white and soft pastels: more exciting
NEUTRALS (Mix of white with brown or black in varying degrees; from pale oyster and ecru to deep browns and flannel grays.)	Low-key and subtle. Lend themselves easily to design changes	Blend readily and can be mixed easily with other colors. Serve as background to decorative elements allowing furnishings to dominate
WHITE	Light and airy. Expands small areas and lightens dark rooms	Will dramatize dark tones or bold colors. Updates a room filled with darker finishes of cherry or mahogany.

TO: ENHANCE FORMALITY AND ELEGANCE: Rich browns, purply blues	CALM AND SOOTHE, CREATE A RESTFUL, COMFORTABLE, RELAXING, AND PEACEFUL ATMOSPHERE: Quiet blues, pale greens, buff, gray, and beige	STIMULATE, PROVOKE, AND EXCITE: Red, yellow, pink—always cheerful but sometimes must be calmed with white

RED

The provocative power of red is seen all around us—in glossy nail lacquer, a cluster of American Beauty roses, a strutting robin's breast, geraniums on a windowsill, quarry tile. For red is indisputably the boldest and bravest of all the colors on the wheel. A small dose will carry far, and an entire room resplendent with red walls, carpeting, even upholstery can be extraordinarily regal and sumptuous. Reds run the gamut from the palest and spiciest pinks to the deepest and most luminous of vermilions, crimsons, and garnets.

Red is not a shy color; it can refresh a room filled with tired furnishings. Neutrals and browns will soften red; white and gold will enhance its elegance. Yellow adds to its liveliness. Pink will pair with red for a deliciously unexpected blend. Red is a traditional color, but it can be utilized to give period rooms contemporary excitement.

YELLOW

The first daffodils of springtime, the silken hair of an ear of corn, butter on a stoneware plate, canaries twittering in a cage—all are variations of lively yellow, irrepressible in its sharper values, rich and mellow in its more burnished aspects. Yellow can transform dark and dismal areas into spots of cheerful sunlight or introduce an unexpected sauciness into a room of neutral shades. Yellow is radiant when teamed with white; black holds yellow down and gives it substance. Bold colors of red and orange make it uncompromisingly boisterous.

BLUE

One of nature's most dependable colors, blue is used as a favored companion to many other colors. Blue is the color of delphiniums and bachelor's buttons, of sapphires and summer berries. The variations seem to be infinite, from the depth of a turquoise Caribbean sea to the clarity of a morning sky. Blue partners white for one of the crispest and most versatile of color combinations, at once lively and serene. Yellow makes blue happier; blue mixes with red and white as one of the most popular color medleys (and the combination for the American flag). Coral, peach, and pink add a delightful sophistication.

ORANGE

Possibly the most exuberant color on the wheel, orange gives us the commonplace objects: tangerines piled in a white bowl, carrots bunched in a garden basket, a child's jack-o'-lantern, a sunset just before dark. Even a little bit of orange can scintillate, can add spice. Orange is mellower when blended with neutrals; it adds a pungent accent to a scheme of browns and blacks. Green expands the garden freshness of orange; blue tempers and tames orange.

GREEN

Green is the favorite color in nature, so it is only natural that we want to use it in all our rooms through plants and flowers, no matter what the color scheme. Green is everywhere outside in the myriad species of trees, plants, and flowers, where an infinite variety of shades blend together in lush harmony. Green is the color of emeralds and malachite, of asparagus and broccoli, of limes and sour apples. In all and any of its shades, green is both exhilarating and soothing. With each partner it demonstrates its extraordinary versatility—with yellow and orange tones, green goes even warmer and becomes more brilliant; blue makes it seem somewhat cooler and more elegant; white heightens its radiance. Green is as evergreen, as much loved and used today, as it was centuries ago, bringing into our homes, even on the bleakest of winter days, the powerful colors of the world outside.

PURPLE

Purple is a strong and regal color when undiluted, and like red, its closest neighbor on the color wheel, it has the power to add regal vibrancy and visual fascination. Tinted or invested with other hues, it develops marvelous, offbeat variations such as plum, eggplant, lavender, periwinkle, hyacinth, orchid. Purple can transform a setting from dull to dazzling, can mix with green for an unpredictable elegance. Neutrals, brown, and black will temper purple; pure purple will lend excitement to white and soft pastels. Modified and muted, purple can be the color of the walls; delicate shades are handsome in a pretty bedroom.

NEUTRALS

As we have said, the first colonists had to be satisfied with the colors of the building materials they used—brick, stone, wood, and plaster. These were neutrals, but neutrals are colors too, to be used as a room's major tones, or to soften and provide a backdrop for one or more brilliant colors. Many people are more comfortable in a room of neutrals. They like the low-key mood that neutrals supply, and if they own colorful paintings, patterned rugs, or furniture in delicate finishes or with exquisite marquetry, they will avoid strong, dominating colors.

A neutral color scheme lends itself to change. Fresh wall paint, a new area rug or draperies, possibly some additional pillows or accessories can be introduced without major re-

Color adds drama: vibrant teal walls set the mood of this elegant apartment dining room.

furbishing. Neutrals run the gamut of colors from pale oyster and ecru shades to deep browns and flannel grays. Neutrals can be mixed together with an easy hand; they blend readily.

WHITE

While neutrals are actually a mix of white with brown or with black in varying degrees, white itself is also a neutral, though one with more clarity. White will dramatize dark tones or bold colors, but it can also stand on its own as the one major color mood of a room. That may sound dull or monotonous, but it seldom is, since white appears totally differently on every texture or material in which it is expressed. The white of a ceramic lamp base is never the white of a velvet fabric, a woven casement cloth, or a lacquered table. White immediately updates a room filled with the darker finishes of cherry or mahogany. White is especially effective in expanding small areas and in lightening dark rooms. With today's stain-resistant finishes, a room done with whites is no longer an exercise in impracticality. And perhaps more important, new synthetics have given us clearer and bolder whites than the whites of some natural materials (which tend to be off-white and usually deepen with age).

There are rules that can guide us in the selection and application of color, for once we have chosen a color scheme, we still have to decide where to apply each color: which one will be the wall tone, which color should be the dominant fabric or carpet hue, and so forth.

One of the safest ways to establish a color scheme is to borrow it from one of the key furnishings you plan to include in the decoration—a wallpaper, a fabric print or pattern, a favorite painting, an Oriental rug, a collection of porcelains. Or, for a room with a lot of outdoor exposure, take the delicious colors that exist in nature (visualize a mixed bouquet of white and yellow tulips, including the green of their stems).

Without any specific kind of color mix such as a wallpaper or fabric print to use as a starting point, one has to develop the scheme from scratch. The most effective and harmonious schemes are either *related* or *complementary*. Related schemes are often monochromatic, variations on a single color—or they are analogous, blending two or more colors adjacent to each other on the wheel (red with yellow and orange, green with blue and violet).

Complementary schemes counterpoint colors that are unlike each other, even opposite each other on the color wheel. Such schemes are often more robust, and usually less muted than related ones. Here it is probably wise to vary the intensities and values of the color used. A paler harmony of blue and peach would obviously be more tender and less intense than the same combination of color applied full strength. The color *mood* you are striving for should determine how powerful each color is to be.

Knowing what colors and color combinations you like, and understanding how to mix and blend them, is certainly a start, but not all that must be grasped about color appreciation before you shape your final color selections.

How a color behaves and what it can accomplish in terms of psychological as well as decorative import are significant considerations. Since color can warm a room, it is mandatory that you assess the climate of the house and the exposure of each room within it. A northern exposure tends to be cool and requires warm colors. So does a room with small windows that bring in little natural light. In the old days when there was no central heating, red carpets, draperies, and bed curtains were used to help people forget how physically cold the room really was.

Color can also cool a room. Again, it's a psychological effect as well as a decorative one. When the sun floods a room with bright and blinding light, you have too much of a good thing. To tame this radiance, or to offer a sense of respite inside a house in a tropical clime, use cool shades of blue and leafy greens. Add pure white to large areas, such as walls and floors.

Color can stimulate, provoke, and excite. Reds, yellows, and pinks are always cheerful, but sometimes are so ebullient they must be calmed with expanses of white or softening neutrals.

Color can calm and soothe. Quiet blues and hushed tones of pale green, buff, gray, and beige are favored for interiors designed as comfortable, restful places within which to work—a home office or library. Studies have demonstrated that these tranquil colors help you relax and feel at ease—the reason they are used in hospital rooms.

Wonderful color—rusts, lemons, limes, and earth tones—is the key to the relaxed lifestyle of the Sun Belt.

Color can enhance the formal or informal style of a room. Purply blues will augment the elegant mood of a dining room. Walls lacquered a rich brown and stripped with white woodwork immediately set a look of dramatic formality. Soft neutrals, on the other hand, allow homespun textures and rough weaves to be easily seen and enjoyed.

Since colors change under different light conditions, you should check out your color choices under both artificial light and daylight. Blues, for example, get bluer under hard bright light; some even turn gray.

Color varies with each texture that expresses it; a color will seem deeper, for instance, in a pile fabric such as velvet than it will in a flat print or weave. Paint takes on one tone when applied to smooth walls, a different value when used on rough-textured backgrounds.

As we have said before, color reacts to color. Any color will seem more intense next to its complement than when viewed alone. Colors look lighter against a dark background, and darker against a pale background. Color can be the focus of attention. If a color scheme concentrates on a single hue or provides a striking and dramatic combination of colors, the color itself is the attention-getter in the room. A rarely publicized tactic of professional designers is to use strong colors as a kind of background support for clients who are themselves somewhat colorless. Such "instant impact" color schemes serve a functional purpose too, as when a home is underfurnished owing to budget limitations. The eye sees only the bold color play, not the paucity of furnishings or the makeshift pieces.

In our discussion of neutral colors, we mentioned that these tones were often desirable for a room rich in exquisitely crafted furniture, a fascinating collection of accessories, or splendid paintings with bold colors of their own. In such cases, subdued colors serve a background role, allowing the furnishings to dominate. A low-key color plan would allow the magnificent wood finishes of such impressive furniture to contribute to the overall color harmony.

Color can unify or divide. By carrying a flow of color from one room to an adjacent room or area, you can visually connect the two and make both seem more spacious. Conversely, a different or contrasting color expressed as wall paint or covering can demarcate one part of a room that is to serve a special purpose, such as a dining area within the main living space.

Once you have understood and digested these color basics and guidelines, you are ready for the most difficult challenge of all: settling on a color scheme and distributing the chosen shades in such a way as to evolve the greatest effectiveness and harmony. It is almost always easier to select a color scheme than it is to apply it; so many possibilities present themselves. Should the blue be used only for the carpeting, or also on the sofa and woodwork? Should the red be limited to a single chair and a few accessories, or also be used for the pillows? White is to be the major color, but to what extent? How does one answer these questions; how does one make the quantum leap from a specific color scheme to a finished room?

Take it one step at a time. First, deal with your backgrounds, primarily floors and walls. Then go on to larger areas, such as sofas, chairs, draperies, and curtains. Finally, select those colors which will appear in pillows, lamps, and other accessories.

To gain maximum interest, you must vary the values, intensities, and areas of the colors to be used. Here are some rules of thumb.

Dominant areas should be in the most neutral colors of the scheme. As the areas decrease in size, the chromatic intensities may be increased proportionately. In other words, the smaller the area, the brighter the color you can use without overpowering the room.

Suppose your color scheme is beige, brown, red, and white with a touch of blue for accent. In a living room you would select a soft tone of beige for the floor, white for the walls—thus using neutrals for the largest expanses. If the room got little natural light, you might (unless practicality were a consideration) consider an even paler color for the floor. If you were using this same scheme in a dining room, however, you might paint the walls red, to create the kind of dramatic mood that sparks conversation, and apply beige and white in draperies, chair seats, and area rugs.

Once you have selected background colors, you are ready for the large upholstered areas and drapery fabrics. Here certain needs must be met. If you want to enlarge the sense of space, then the drapery fabric should be the same color as the walls. For a more dynamic effect, you might cover the sofa in a fabric that contrasts with the carpet color. For a smaller room, however, you would probably choose different colors for the sofa and carpet, but similar values or tones for each color, so that the contrast would not be marked.

In arranging the secondary color or colors to be used for medium-sized areas, try to achieve balance. Do not use all the strong or vivid tones on one side of the room; if you do put a bold drapery print at the window, repeat it for balance in pillows, a large chair, or a skirted table elsewhere in the room.

Before selecting accessories, it is sometimes a good idea to wait until walls have been painted and secondary areas have been filled in. For these "accents" can then be utilized to compensate for whatever additional color "hype" the room might need, or else tone down a setting where the color scheme might become flamboyant with accents other than in white or neutral tones.

Many woods may exist in a single room in a variety of furniture finishes, and usually this is more desirable than finding matching tables and cabinets—for a diversity of color tone creates more vitality. But then you may discover, after your walls have been painted, the carpeting put down, the sofa, chairs, cabinets, and table positioned, that the room is much darker than you had anticipated, owing to this mix of woods. Therefore, you might, in such cases, use softer colors in accents and accessories.

A word about color flow and continuity. In a small apartment you would certainly want or need to continue the basic color scheme throughout (with some variations from room to room) in order to provide a greater sense of space. Even in a large house, you should avoid the shock of too much contrast, as can happen when you walk from one room into another that has been interpreted in an entirely different color plan. There should always be a color relationship between adjacent areas, even though the most prominent color in one room plays only a minor role in the other. To achieve a sense of harmony and spatial flow, you must have color discipline.

In selecting and distributing your color scheme, be a little daring. Instead of playing it safe with the same tried-and-true color combinations you've lived with in other houses or apartments, try a new and truly fresh color plan, though one that is personally comfortable rather than trendy. Set your goals, follow the guidelines, but then give yourself some room for self-expression.

A painter does not know at the start what colors he will use to fill his canvas and just where he will add them, although he has some general plan. You too must work within a discipline, yet have the courage to bring in your own ideas as you go about the task of coloring your home.

Getting a decorating project off the ground is often the most difficult part of the procedure. Even with a clear idea of the ultimate goal to be achieved, how does one begin? The choices are

CHAPTER 4
WHERE TO START AND HOW TO PLAN

innumerable, the possibilities endless. There is certainly more than one way to create a rustic American dining room, or a handsome living room that mixes contemporary upholstery with Queen Anne–style tables and cabinets.

Fortunately, few decorating jobs start entirely from scratch. Usually we are blessed at the start with a handful of possessions and furnishings—perhaps a much-cherished family heirloom, or a few good holdovers from another apartment—that can provide the cornerstone for our decorating project.

It is hardly sensible, however, to design an entire room, let alone a complete house, around a collection of furnishings that no longer satisfy one's needs or fit smoothly into a proposed style and room-arrangement plan. Here one must be willing to eliminate the negative and sell off or give away possessions that are neither suitable, attractive, or durable enough to work in the new interiors, even though they may still hold some sentimental value. On the other hand, a wonderful Oriental rug, a few treasured paintings, a superb antique china cabinet, a favorite old brass bedstead might be worth keeping and using as a starting base.

The decorating plan, in such cases, would then work out an arrangement that incorporates these cherished possessions

Ceramic collectibles, based on barnyard themes, give a starting point to a cozy and colorful country dining room that blends informal maple and pine designs.

A DESIGN CONCEPT CAN BEGIN WITH . . .

- furniture and accessories you have selected to keep

- precious pieces you've dreamed of owning

- specific patterns, textures, or prints of wall covering

- collectibles

- one necessary object that may determine the purpose and layout of the room (like twin beds)

- a dominant architectural feature of the room

- making the best of an architectural disadvantage

into the overall scheme so that they look as if they really belonged, not like a carryover from another life. The tones of the Oriental rug could be repeated in upholstery and other fabric colors. A seating group could be centered around the large cabinet. The collection of paintings might be mixed with new acquisitions, and placed in a totally fresh and fascinating wall composition in one of the living or dining areas.

So assess the furniture and accessories you've inherited, accumulated, and still love as a way of giving direction to your plan. Once you have decided which ones will work and which must be discarded, you can use the viable choices to get your scheme going.

You can also start off your decorating plan with possessions you own only in your mind's eye, but have been determined to purchase once you could afford them, or had sufficient space. For years you may have hungered for a set of pierced-splat-back dining chairs, or a broken-pediment highboy for a bedroom, or have dreamed of purchasing a camel-back Chippendale sofa, a collection of red-and-white quilts, a painted corner cabinet, a hutchful of spongeware. Whether you realized it or not, here are some potential starting points.

Another excellent way to begin a decorating project is with a specific pattern or print, one that may exist in a wallpaper, a drapery or upholstery fabric, a carpet or rug, a collection of pillows. This is an almost foolproof way of carrying through a color plan. If you start with a wallpaper for your bedroom, for instance, you can simply pick out the colors within its design and apply them to bed linens, carpeting, curtains, and accessories. So if you have decided that wallpaper is to be used in a room, select this first, and the rest of the plan will follow easily. For example, if you have chosen a texture or pattern that is muted or small in scale, you can use bolder patterns and prints in the same room. On the other hand, if you have selected a boldly patterned and colored wall covering, you will probably confine your other choices to plain textures and more subdued colors.

Stencil-look fabric print established the color plan of this city living
room that has a sophisticated yet unmistakable country style.

These same considerations apply when you start with a drapery print or an upholstered fabric. These patterns not only will supply the color scheme, but will also determine how many other designs can be used in the same room and where they will be expressed. If all your upholstered furniture is to be covered in the same vibrant, large-scale floral print, for example, you will need to play down color and pattern on walls and in the floor covering.

Carpets and area rugs, once considered to be merely background accoutrements, often play a major decorating role in today's interiors, especially if they are patterned, or boast a vivid mix of colors, or consist of a single, brilliant hue. Other furnishings should then be planned around this dazzling starting point.

If you own an extensive collection of artifacts—redware, for example, or antique baskets, majolica, American folk art, stoneware jugs, or decoys, you will have to provide for ample cabinetry shelves and tabletops that will both organize and display it for maximum impact. Such requirements will affect the kind of storage designs you include in your floor plan and where you place them. To show off your collections, you may prefer to use open-shelf hutches instead of cabinets with closed doors, or you may choose other kinds of furniture designs that offer ample shelf space, such as book-stack units. Or you might have to plan for a certain amount of built-in shelf area.

The starting points we have described so far have been those which offer color, shape, design, and mood. In some instances, however, you may have to build a decorating plan around a necessary object, rather than upon an aesthetic choice. This could be a dual-purpose sleep sofa, a pair of twin beds, a copious array of audio and video equipment, or a triple dresser for a sizable wardrobe. Once you have zeroed in on any such "musts" for the various rooms of your home, you can use them as starting points of the plan. A sofa that converts to a bed in a studio apartment would require a coffee table in front of it that is light enough to be moved easily out of the way at bedtime; it would also re-

The Oriental mood of this small living area was initially inspired by the large decorative coffee table, a contemporary interpretation of a Chinese Chippendale design.

quire a fabric cover that is sturdy and unlikely to soil. Twin beds might limit the selection of other furniture, such as nightstands and dressers, in a bedroom of modest size, as would the essential triple dresser. To house your electronic equipment, you would need the kind of furniture specifically designed for this purpose, or else count on deep and adequate shelf space. Setting aside part of your bedroom or living room to serve as a home office would be another living essential that could give direction to the plan.

Very few of us, amateur or professional, can execute a decorating project for which money is no object. Critical to any budget, large or small, is the use of decorating dollars in the most efficient ways, to make the money really count. This search for efficiency and effectiveness in spending can also offer a starting point. For once you have estimated what your budget is to be, you will next have to decide how to allocate what is available—where to spend more, where to economize. This kind of allotment process may persuade you to choose wall paint instead of wall covering or to purchase area rugs instead of entailing the expense of installing wall-to-wall carpeting. So, too, can ready-made curtains and draperies present themselves as a less costly alternative to custom-made window treatments.

Try to stretch the dollar where you can. Don't make your starting points so expensive that they become finishing points as well. Control the impulse to put most of your budget into a fabulous rug or sumptuous silk wall coverings if this means you will have to live with orange crates until more money is accumulated. Just as foolish is the opposite tack: buying inexpensive, short-lived furniture that achieves the look of a completely furnished home, but will not stand up to wear and tear over the long run. Buy what you need and can afford now, limiting yourself to furnishings that have value and promise long-range durability. Even if you have to create rooms that are at first somewhat incomplete, you can always fill in later, as long as there is an established design plan for you to follow.

An Oriental rug initiated the mood of quiet elegance in this handsome library. Upholstery and wall colors are all "pulled" from rug tones.

HOW TO PLAN YOUR HOME

There is no substitute for careful planning to ensure that your home will function and look the way you see it in your dreams. Planning may take time, thought, and energy, but it doesn't cost a cent. In fact, a plan can save you a great deal of money by helping you avoid disastrous purchases made on impulse. If you stick to your plan, you'll be less likely to run out of money for something that's desperately needed for a basic arrangement. Working with a blueprint as you go about purchasing the different furnishings, you will have a clear idea of what you can afford, what you need to buy today, what can be purchased at a later date, and so on. You'll find it that much easier to make decisions in stores that offer a dizzying multitude of choices.

It's vital to the success of your decorating plan that you understand what you are basically trying to do. Remember that your home is for living and that aesthetic preferences aside, the major goals should be comfort, convenience, atmosphere or mood, and specific living needs—such as facilities for sleeping, sitting, dining, storage, and so on.

Comfort is a vital factor in most decorating decisions. You and your family should feel completely at ease as you perform the many activities that are part of your home life. This means having a place to put up your feet; it means owning chairs, sofas, and bedding that feel as good as they look. Before you buy upholstery or bedding, test it out—sit in it; lie on it (more on this in our chapter on furniture).

Comfort also means providing adequate light to work or read by. It means choosing colors and patterns that are pleasing rather than disconcerting.

Convenience is another important goal. Having plenty of easily accessible storage space is certainly a prime convenience, because it allows the room to store and organize assorted belongings and precludes the need to constantly search for lost possessions.

Atmosphere or mood—the overall feeling and ambiance of an interior—is another goal. This mood can be serene, vibrant, formal, or casual—to name a few possibilities. Creating atmosphere calls for more planning than cash; the key is simply in knowing what the mood is to be and how to establish it. There's a lot on creating moods in the previous chapter on color, and in later chapters on accessories.

A plan for decorating your home usually doesn't just occur to you; it evolves. We have talked about all the possible starting points that make it easier to get a project off to a good beginning, but you must also think in terms of satisfying basic living needs, the activities endemic to human life in a home: sleeping, eating, dressing, washing, relaxing, entertaining, and work or study. If you examine each of these

The spectacular architectural features of this two-story living room encouraged the design of one large seating group and the dazzling all-white color scheme.

Chippendale camel-back love seat is the centerpiece around which this adaptation of an 18th-century parlor was designed.

in terms of every member of your family, you will have a foundation for your essential requirements.

Sleeping, for example, demands a separate bed for every family member, except couples. A good bed is a major purchase, and if you are starting from scratch, a bed should be among the first things you buy.

When you shop for a bed, consider both comfort and support. Although most mattresses are labeled with such descriptive terms as "firm," "medium firm," and "extra firm," there are no industry standardizations of these terms; for all practical purposes they are meaningless. So you have to make your own judgments, and the only way to do this is to try out each mattress in the store and buy from a reputable retailer and manufacturer who will stand behind the product.

If you have a large house with a separate bedroom for each single person in the family, you're unlikely to have problems deciding where the beds will go. On the other hand, placing a bed can be a major decorating challenge in a one-room studio apartment. Also, if children share a bedroom, your plan must take this special situation into account, so that each child's needs are satisfied. (More on this in the chapter on bedrooms.)

Eating at home is an activity that occurs once, twice, or three times a day. Snacking is even more frequent. Each abode requires one dining table with enough space and chairs for every living-in member of the family. If your home is so small as to lack a separate dining area, you will have to solve the dilemma of where to put that table. If your home is spacious, and you have occasions to eat in other places than the kitchen or dining room, you will want to incorporate other opportune dining locations (such as a foyer or living-room alcove) into your overall plan.

Dressing is an activity that requires more storage space than anything else. You will need dresser and closet space for in-season and off-season clothes. You will also need a place to store your toiletries, and for proper mirror and lighting facilities in your bathroom and dressing areas.

Washing should be a fairly simple need to solve, since most houses and apartments contain at least one bathroom, with tub and/or shower and sink. But you must wash your clothes as well. If space permits, you can install your own washer and dryer; if not, you will need adequate container space for dirty laundry that accumulates to be taken to the Laundromat.

Does your house or apartment have such excellent storage space as huge walk-in closets, storage or cedar closets, a usable attic, a roomy basement; or must most of your possessions and clothing be contained in dressers and cabinets? If the latter is the case, this will certainly affect your choice of furniture (as will be discussed in greater detail in our chapters on furniture choice and arrangement).

The characteristics of each of your rooms affect the way it looks and functions. Take a walk through your home and make a visual study. You probably already know what you like and don't like about each and every room, but have you thought about the role each room must play and how its special features affect the activities carried on there?

Be flexible about the role each room has to serve. The fact that a builder or architect has labeled one room a living room, another a dining room, a third a family room doesn't mean you have to use these rooms that way. Open up your mind to a wider range of possibilities. By switching room roles, you can often make a house or apartment's space serve your needs more satisfactorily.

Some examples of such role reversals: Turn a dining room into a needed extra bedroom. Let a foyer serve for dining. Use a dining ell as a sleeping area for a new baby. Trans-

Rich pine woods of dining furniture create an updated keeping room in a contemporary house.

form a family room into a space where many hobbies are enjoyed or a home office that runs from 9 to 5. Design a library that is also a hidden guest room.

Take inventory and make a realistic budget. Also assess the amount of time, skill, and energy you and your family will have to invest in the execution of your design plan. Labor today often costs as much as or more than materials, so try to ascertain how much time you can devote to home projects yourself and how long it will take you to complete them. If you're inexperienced, build some extra time into the estimate. Go through the house and analyze each room vis-à-vis these considerations. If you have enough time and are willing to go slowly, then decide whether you really have the energy and talent to do it yourself. Some projects can be completed in an evening, while others require several weekends. One or two costly mistakes, and an inept do-it-yourselfer's attempts to cut corners on professional help can prove disastrous.

There are many factors that will and must be considered at the very start of your decorating job. Try to cover all bases, and satisfy all the more important priorities. Above all, take your time at the planning stage; it will pay off and make the entire process that much faster in the long run.

PART TWO
ELEMENTS OF DECOR-ATION

Unless you are building a house entirely from scratch, you have little or no control over the structural design of and materials used for your apartment or house. The background elements—walls, windows, floors, ceilings, fireplaces, fixed openings, and architectural ornamentation—are all there when you move in. The challenge of decorating is to enhance the assets among these elements and to cope with or camouflage the liabilities.

The skillful handling of floor, wall, and window decoration is critical to the design of any room, because these areas are so large and so conspicuous. What would be a mere mistake in the choice of a lamp or a pillow would here be a major disaster. It is also essential that in addition to creating attractive and well-planned backgrounds for your furnishings, you use all the decorating tools at your disposal to compensate for a room's poor or awkward proportions, its low ceiling or undersized, off-balance windows. You must also find a way of dealing with unwelcome architectural protrusions, alcoves, and recesses, and of renewing scarred or blemished floors and walls. Unless you eliminate these eyesores, they will undermine the beauty of the furnishings you put in your rooms, no matter how attractive the arrangement.

A well-designed background is like the backdrop of a stage—able to stand on its own before a single actor has entered the set. A room bare of furniture, but beautifully embellished with paint and wallpaper, a compatible window treatment, and a floor of luxurious texture or resplendent with a luminous Oriental rug will be a pleasing place to stand in. The backgrounds of your own rooms should be attractive enough to pass this test.

With these backgrounds settled, you will want to know next the various furniture designs to consider as components most compatible and pleasing against and within your backdrops—the *living* components of your decoration.

The early colonists built their houses right over bare earth, using wood planks, stone, and later bricks to give their interiors the necessary flooring. These natural materials continue to be popular

CHAPTER 5
FLOOR COVERINGS

choices for today's rooms that emulate the style and mood of Colonial houses; but there are many other ways to treat the floor of an interior decorated with American Traditional furnishings.

Your choice of floor treatment will be influenced by the style of the interior, the purposes you wish the floor covering to serve, the size of your room, the proposed furniture arrangement, and the likely traffic patterns. You have three basic options: uncovered, smooth-surfaced floors; carpeted floors; and smooth floors decorated with large or small area rugs.

A heavy-duty enamel paint and layers of polyurethane overcoat can restore a floor that is scarred but not really damaged, giving a fresh sweep of bright contemporary or soft traditional color. If your floors are badly damaged, you can have them repaired and refinished, or you can cover them up with a blanket of wall-to-wall carpeting. Carpeting the floor would also be suitable if you wanted to insulate your room against noise or cold, or if you preferred the warmth and decorative dimension of a texture, or needed to unify chopped-up areas and enlarge small spaces.

Perhaps you intend to create a very decorative look by arranging your furniture in independent groups, set out in the middle of the room rather than against its perimeter. In this instance you could demarcate or anchor these conversation

The formal style of this imposing blue-and-white area carpet matches the elegance of a living room furnished with Sheraton, Hepplewhite, and Duncan Phyfe furniture.

arrangements with patterned area rugs placed under the furniture groups and framed by highly polished floors that add luster and a reflective element to your backdrop.

Rooms broken up with alcoves, recesses, and numerous fixed openings often need the integrating force of carpeting installed wall-to-wall. So do multilevel areas whose plywood platforms require the concealing cover of a durable texture.

Your floor covering can play anything from a minor to a major role in the room's decoration. Muted carpeting in a monochromatic scheme is never conspicuous, but its texture, warmth, and presence are clearly felt. An area rug in a dazzling color or dynamic pattern can dominate a room visually and emotionally. Area rugs or carpets of subtle color, texture, and design do not fade into the background when furniture is added, but neither do they steal the scene.

The roles that a room is required or apt to play will also dictate the choice of floor coverings. Bedrooms are popular areas for wall-to-wall carpeting, which provides a warm cushion for the inevitable bare feet. Kitchens, bathrooms, and utility rooms are usually paved with a smooth, easy-to-clean covering such as ceramic tile, vinyl tile, or vinyl sheeting.

If you dream of re-creating the mood of an authentic Colonial home, you will most likely select braided or rag rugs for the humbler interiors, elegant Orientals for the more formal settings. But if you wish to update your traditional furniture with some contemporary design or color elements, you could use area rugs of solid texture or carved border design, or go with wall-to-wall carpeting in a fresh, bright hue.

The degree of formality or informality to be established will also guide you in making selections. A hooked rug would support the flavor of a rustic keeping room. Textured carpeting would work best in a casual family room or den. A tight, velvety weave would enhance the sense of luxury in an elegant living room.

The colors, textures, and finishes of floor coverings should be practical enough to stand up to whatever wear and tear may be expected of that area, whether from heavy usage, well-defined traffic lanes, children and pets, or frequent entertaining, if that is your style.

While you are collecting ideas for wall paint, wallpaper, upholstery, and drapery fabrics, you should also be adding samples of textured and smooth floor coverings to each

FLOOR SURFACES

TYPE OF SURFACE	STRENGTH
I. SOFT SURFACE: Oriental Rugs: Persian, Turkish, Turkoman, Indian, Caucasian, Chinese	Any of these Orientals will accent the beauty and formality of any room; especially favorable in a Chippendale dining room
Area Rugs: Braided and rag rugs and hooked rugs	Can provide center for a seating arrangement, tie together a color plan, or inspire a plan. Can also define separate areas of activity within the same room
Carpeting: Wall-to-wall and room-sized rugs, from thick velvet plush to nubby, low-level tightly woven or looped textures	Insulates and decorates. Provides warmth, cushions against noise, unifies broken areas, relates adjacent rooms, extends the look of a monochromatic color scheme
II. SYNTHETIC SMOOTH SURFACE Vinyl	Perfect for rooms that get heavy traffic
Asphalt	Practical and inexpensive
Terrazzo Rubber Linoleum	Highly durable and easy to maintain
Cork	Resilient and insulating
III. NATURAL-MATERIAL SMOOTH SURFACE Wood	The beauty of the grain will accent and enhance any interior
Ceramic Tile	Easy to clean, perfect for kitchens and bathrooms
Brick Slate	Gives the flavor and mood of an old-time Colonial home
Marble	Luxurious for any room; perfect for foyer or small dining area

room's portfolio of swatches and clippings. Your selections for any one room should fit together like the pieces of a jigsaw puzzle. They are interrelated, in that the final choice of any single element must be made within the framework of other choices, never alone.

The precise design of that Colonial favorite, the hooked rug, made from scraps of yarn, is emulated here in a large area rug manufactured with modern loom technology and synthetic fibers.

AMERICAN TRADITIONAL

Today's machine-made version of the braided rug comes through in a specific color theme, rather than the hit-and-miss effect that resulted from whatever rags were utilized by frugal colonists.

AREA RUGS

Patterned carpets, or area rugs as they are popularly referred to today, encompass a broad range of styles.

In recent years, the emphasis by professionals on a more decorative and personal approach to floor covering has virtually exploded the catalogues of area-rug design and broadened the source list. Oriental rugs are meticulously copied by American manufacturers. Disparate countries such as Greece and Finland now make new versions of American rag rugs.

Among other favored designs to surface recently are needlepoints from France and Portugal, richly textured patterns from Scandinavia and North Africa, flat Dhurries and Kilims from India and the Middle East. The geometric patterns and soft pastel colorations of these popular Dhurries give them enormous versatility, with styles that can enrich any setting from period traditional to upbeat contemporary.

The area rugs that are considered to be most compatible with American Traditional furnishings are quite naturally those designs first developed in Colonial times. Like so many of our most cherished and enduring handcrafts, Colonial rugs were born of necessity. Frugal colonists did not have the money or materials to spend on essentials, let alone luxuries, so those all-time Colonial standbys, braided rugs, rag rugs, and hooked rugs, were fashioned out of scraps of materials and odd bits of yarn.

Resourceful New Englanders crafted the material for braided rugs out of any piece of fabric they could get their hands on, sewing these remnants into long strands which were then braided and sewn into oval or round shapes. Today, American manufacturers and importers offer machine-made versions of these handcrafted rugs, usually made with a filler for extra wear, and often in precise color varieties rather than the hit-and-miss effects that materialized from Colonial scraps. New manufactured and sometimes handmade versions of these Colonial favorites are executed in eighteenth-century colorations, but are also produced in fresh, brilliant new adaptations. They can even be found as broadloom, to be installed in a room wall-to-wall when a complete cover is required.

Rag rugs were another Colonial economy, and as the name indicates were crafted from assorted rags and bits of fabric sewn into strands and woven on a hand loom. The coloring of a handmade Colonial rag rug was striated, and as random as the materials from which it was made. Current fascination with these rugs, for use in contemporary as well as farmhouse American rooms, has led to reinterpretation as well. Today's versions are often in one solid color shaded by subtle striations, or come in completely unpredictable combinations of fresh, sizzling hues. Importers have been encouraged to develop cottage industries around the globe that provide a constant flow of fresh variations. Colonial colors are often emulated, but the bold and brilliant mixes with contemporary flair are more abundant.

Hooked rugs, made from yarn worked into a canvas backing with a hooking needle, offer a precise design or motif, rather than the allover, mottled colorations of the braids and rag rugs. Colonial floral and block patterns and charming folk art motifs are among the more familiar designs. People who enjoy needlework can even hook their own rugs, for the process is a relatively simple and speedy one. Another option is to buy rugs manufactured to resemble the look of a hooked rug, but with motifs sometimes expressed in cut as well as looped pile.

ORIENTAL RUGS

Technically, an Oriental rug is any rug handmade in Asia. It doesn't have to be old, beautiful, or valuable, although to be considered an antique it must be at least one hundred years old.

The first Orientals, made by nomads some three thousand or more years ago, were among their owners' more important possessions; they served a variety of purposes—for lean-tos; as tent doors; piled up to make sofas, chairs, and beds; laid out flat for dining surfaces. All the nomad's belongings traveled with him in his carpet; supposedly Cleopatra was delivered to Caesar rolled up in an Oriental rug.

About the time that wood furniture became a status symbol for the Parisians, Oriental rugs became a sign of affluence in European homes. Among the earliest Orientals were the Turkish prayer rugs, which even today are made with the traditional arched prayer niche (*mihab*) or similar directional signal to point toward Mecca.

Traditional Oriental rugs were made of sheep's wool, cotton, goat hair, silk, and in one period, linen. They were usually named for the village or area where they were made. The six major classifications today for Oriental rugs are Persian (from Iran), Turkish, Turkoman (made by nomadic tribes of Central Asia), Indian, Caucasian, and Chinese.

Oriental rugs in Europe were so highly valued at first that they were used as table covers, and did not become floor coverings until the eighteenth century. Today's passion for using Orientals in modern rooms as well as in period settings has caused their prices to soar, but many manufacturers make close adaptations of these handmades which provide a virtually indistinguishable appearance at a much lower price tag.

Two other rugs that should be mentioned in connection with Orientals are Aubussons and Savonneries. Both come from France but began with designs borrowed from the Orient. Aubussons date back to the Middle Ages, and Savonneries were first seen in the seventeenth century. The muted pastel colorings and floral designs characteristic of these rug genres have also been adapted to machine-made, more reasonably priced versions. Their patterns are quite elegant in style and are more suited to formal interiors.

DECORATING WITH AREA RUGS AND ORIENTALS

Area rugs not only act as a center for a seating arrangement, but also serve to tie together a color plan or even inspire the color plan chosen for a room.

A dining arrangement gains from the punctuation of an area rug, which anchors the furniture and lends color and pattern to a room usually dominated by the wood finishes of its furniture—table, chairs, and cabinets. In a dining room, the area rug should always extend beyond the point reached by the dining chairs when they are pulled out. Living-room seating arrangements, on the other hand, can be placed beyond the rug to stand on the smooth flooring.

Pale or lightly and brightly colored area rugs can enliven a dark corner of a room, or any space that receives little natural light. Area rugs also define separate areas of activity within the same interior, such as living and dining, sitting and study. An area rug also may provide the major or only strong pattern and color in a room of solid fabrics and neu-

Oriental rugs were a favorite anchor for more formal 18th-century rooms. Here, a modern version holds together an intimate seating arrangement.

tral tones. The proportions of an area rug can be used to create a mood of intimacy in a room that may be too spacious; often more than one area rug and furniture arrangement are used to visually divide an oversized space.

Area rugs that come in almost solid colors, such as those with carved designs and borders, or the popular Berber and sisal textures, have a strong architectural character and are just as flexible as plain-colored wall-to-wall carpeting. Area rugs, however, can be rotated to avoid the wear and tear of traffic lanes. They also offer greater flexibility when moving time comes, and they are easier and less costly to have cleaned.

Not only do today's area rugs come in many diverse designs and textures; they are often seen in innovative shapes such as hexagonal, octagonal, and, on occasion, free-form.

CARPETING

Carpeting is a term that usually refers to broadloom, a texture woven or tufted in widths of 9, 12, 15, and 18 feet. Carpeting has several special qualities: color flexibility; ease of care; heat, cold, and sound insulation; safety; and thick texture underfoot.

Broadloom carpeting used to be much more expensive than it is today, because it was manufactured exclusively of wool and woven on costly Axminster, Wilton, and Velvet looms, machines owned and operated by a handful of mills. But then modern technology developed the fast and economical tufting process, and a wide range of synthetic fibers with exceptional durability, soil resistance, and color clarity brought broadloom carpeting within the price range of all. Today's new broadlooms are significantly less costly than the quality broadlooms of thirty years ago, inflation notwithstanding.

FIBER CHART

FIBER	DURABILITY	SOIL & STAIN RESISTANCE	COLOR CLARITY	OTHER SPECIAL CHARACTERISTICS
WOOL	Good	Not as good as many synthetics	Takes dye well	Soft, lustrous, long-wearing
NYLON	Excellent	Resists stains; easy to clean	Easily dyed in manufacture; available in spectrum of colors	Especially good for families with small children
POLYESTERS	Good	More susceptible to oil-based stains & soils	Good	Offer excellent crush resistance
ACRYLICS	Fair	Resist stains fairly well	Good	Light and bulky; feel like wool
OLEFINS	Poor	Resist staining & abrasions quite well	Resist fading; poor dying potential	Especially good for kitchens and as indoor/outdoor carpeting

For care and cleaning of carpeting, the sooner you remove a spill, the less chance there is of staining. It is best to use a white terry towel. If there is any residue after the towel soaks up the liquid, mix one teaspoon of mild detergent and one teaspoon of white vinegar in a quart of water. Sponge or brush the solution into the carpet pile and remove by blotting with paper towels or clean cloths.

Melon-colored wall-to-wall carpeting blends with matching wall tone to provide this large bedroom with a monochromatic backdrop.

Carpeting should be installed wall-to-wall only in homes where the family plans to stay put. The amount of waste that occurs when a carpet is cut to cover a floor exactly, as well as the cost of installation, makes wall-to-wall a sizable investment that is impractical unless it can be amortized over a period of time. For homes or apartments that are likely to be temporary, it makes more sense to use broadloom in room-size rugs. These carpets can be picked up easily and reassigned to new roles when it's time to move.

Carpet textures run the gamut from smooth, densely woven velvets to craggier effects. The fad for shags, once the hit of the marketplace, has subsided in recent seasons; this was to be expected of a fashion trend that was an exaggerated version of a textural look. Today's most popular broadloom is the thick velvet plush. Nubbier textures for casual room settings, and low-level, tightly woven looped constructions for stairways, landings, and high-traffic areas are in great demand as well. There are also carpets that offer monochromatic patterns in random sheared effects and multilevel looped textures.

It is a fairly easy matter to gauge a carpet's potential for elegance by observing its texture: smooth velvet plushes enhance a room's formality; rough textures enforce a more casual look.

Style and construction do not alone determine the quality of carpeting. Density and height of pile and type of fiber and backing are other factors that affect the value and price of a specific texture.

A generation ago, wall-to-wall carpeting was considered as much of a status symbol as a new mink coat. Today, there is more emphasis on personal, less anonymous floor treatment. But wall-to-wall is still eminently preferable and effective for certain purposes.

Wall-to-wall carpeting insulates, integrates, and decorates. It provides warmth underfoot, eliminates the noisy "clop-clop" of high heels on smooth floors, and generally acts as a buffer or softening agent to noise within or without the home. As a flowing blanket of color it can unify chopped-up areas, relate two adjacent rooms, and supply the major portion of vibrant, dark, warm, pale, or subtle color to a room, thereby heightening or toning down the decorating scheme. And as we suggested earlier, wall-to-wall is especially desirable in bedrooms, where so many of us walk around barefoot and enjoy the softness and warmth of thickly covered floors.

Wall-to-wall carpeting can create a flow of color from one area to another, such as from a living room to a study alcove, a dining room to a tiny entry area, a sleeping alcove to a major living area. Not only does this flow of color lend a sense of continuity between these areas; it also enhances their overall feeling of space.

Carpeting can add bright and light colors to compensate for the dark woods of furniture or paneling. It can spell the difference between a dull and a dazzling room by repeating one of the pattern colors in a sofa or drapery print rather than continuing the off-white or muted tone of the background color. If a drapery or upholstery print or pattern is exceptionally brilliant or strong, however, softly colored carpeting can tone down the effect. Carpeting can also implement the look of a monochromatic scheme more effectively than any other design element.

Carpeting creates mood by the way it colors a room and adds that extra dimension of luxury or rough-hewn texture. It can support a sense of quiet and serenity; dramatize a lively, vibrant mood; or invest an interior with a wonderful elegance or feeling of cozy warmth and intimacy. So keep mood-creating quality in mind when purchasing new carpeting to replace some that is worn out, especially if you wish to give a specific look to an interior whose floor has been handled in a totally different way.

SMOOTH-SURFACED FLOORING

Today's open approach to decorating does not single out one floor-covering treatment as more attractive or effective than any other. What is always critical to the choice is the role or roles the floor treatment must serve. Smooth floors, used with or without area rugs, are another wonderful element for contemporary or American Traditional interiors.

As we mentioned earlier, the first colonists covered their earthen floors with plain boards and later, when they were able to extract color out of nature, made them more decorative with coats of paint. In addition to painting boards, they eventually developed other handcrafts to enhance and decorate their flooring. They discovered the art of comb painting—using a comb with wide teeth to create a ribbed crosshatch design on the wet paint. Stenciling was also used to give painted floors allover motifs and/or a hand-painted border design.

Hand-painted floor cloths, a popular and economical device, are another Colonial craft that has been revived as contemporary art. Today's fresh versions are given wear-worthy coats of polyurethane over their painted designs.

Comb painting—an easy and colorful way to cover uninteresting or blemished wood floors. Floor is given a coat of paint and then combed with a notched squeegee. Protective coats of clear polyurethane are then applied. When it's finished, a wonderful look is achieved for a country dining room with fabric-covered walls and Windsor chairs.

Pegged, random-width flooring, a favorite base in Colonial homes, is now manufactured in assorted woods and finishes and can be used to replace a badly scarred or damaged floor or simply to establish the suitable underpinnings for a Colonial interior. For a more formal effect, parquet flooring can be installed. It is also possible to enhance the wood floors you now possess by hiring a professional to stain and refinish them. If you are ambitious enough and handy, you can rent the equipment and renew the floors yourself.

Wood floors and other floors of either natural or synthetic materials are obvious decorating candidates in areas that get a tremendous amount of wear such as halls, foyers and entries, and dining rooms. An easy-care floor is especially essential in a dining room which occasionally suffers the spills of food and beverages. Some larger floors will require a more practical base, as well as the softening texture or bold counterpoint of an area rug. This play of smooth and rough or luxurious texture adds visual and tactile interest to a room.

Here is a breakdown of the more popular smooth floorings:

WOOD: A highly polished wood floor covered with Orientals or left bare is the last word in beauty for those who love the exquisite graining and mellow tones of wood. Wood floors also grow more beautiful as they age—the reason their popularity has sustained the test of time. The most popular woods are oak and maple, but cherry, walnut, teak, pecan, beech, and birch are also favored. Wood floors can be protected with regular waxing or more permanently coated with a protective finish of polyurethane.

CERAMIC TILE: Offered today in either glazed textures or unglazed terra cotta, ceramic tiles are available in just about every color, design, and size. Increasingly, these tiles are being used for rooms other than bathrooms. Very easy to wash clean, but not as resilient underfoot as wood or synthetic floorings, they must be installed with a grout that can either match or be in a contrasting color. Ceramic tiles are popular in hexagonal and rectangular as well as square shapes.

BRICK AND SLATE: Brick can be purchased new; old brick can be readily found at outlets that specialize in salvaged building materials. Not the most comfortable flooring underfoot, brick does convey the mood of an old-time Colonial keeping room as no other flooring can. Today slate comes precut and is offered in an assortment of colors. Both these materials are extremely durable and easy to keep clean (if given a polyurethane finish), but they have no resilience and are best used in small areas, or in rooms where a special flavor is desired.

MARBLE: A marble floor sounds like the last word in luxury, and indeed it is, though marble today is made in thinner pieces that considerably reduce its cost. While marble will stain easily, it has a unique character expressed in variegated textural effects and colorings. An entry hall or small dining room, where a limited amount would be required, might be the place to splurge on marble. A quick washing cleans off surface dirt and grime.

SYNTHETIC SMOOTH SURFACES

The high cost of wood and other natural flooring materials prompted the building-supply industry to develop a new floor material: vinyl. Today vinyl is one of the most important and commonly used smooth floorings in the American home. This kind of flooring and other developments in synthetics, all of them no more than a generation old, have revolutionized the flooring industry.

VINYL: Available both as a tile and in sheeting, vinyl is made in clear, brilliant colors that can be used in more upscale areas—such as a black-and-white checkerboard floor for a dining room, or a soft pastel under a large area rug in a bedroom. Vinyl sheeting with inlaid designs that emulate such natural materials as brick, marble, terrazzo, and, most especially, ceramic tile is often an automatic choice for kitchens, utility rooms, mud rooms, playrooms, and other areas that get a lot of hard wear.

Some sheet vinyl comes with its own cushioned backing. Not all sheeting can be installed on grade, so check out any vinyl you intend to buy. New, more supple vinyl sheeting and easy-to-handle vinyl tile are especially suitable for do-it-yourself projects.

VINYL ASBESTOS: Inexpensive and ideal for on-grade installation, vinyl asbestos is porous, stain-resistant, durable, and easy to keep clean. It resists dents, but has no resilience or noise absorption.

ASPHALT: This low-cost and very practical flooring goes on grade, but dents easily and is not resistant to grease.

OTHER SMOOTH FLOORINGS

TERRAZZO: Made of natural materials—stone or marble chips—terrazzo is a man-made composite with a unique pattern and texture. Highly durable, it is very easy to take care of.

RUBBER: Once a very popular flooring because of its resilience, rubber has been replaced by the lower-cost vinyl. Dents bounce back quickly, but rubber can stain.

CORK: Its unique texture and high resilience still make cork a favorite for certain informal rooms, especially playrooms. It is also a superb insulator against noise.

LINOLEUM: Once a top market product, linoleum has been replaced by vinyl sheeting, although it is still offered by many firms as a practical and low-cost material. Linoleum sheeting is very durable and easy to maintain, but should not be used on grade or below grade.

$\mathbf{W}$alls define the size
and shape of a room, articulating the nooks and crannies,
the protrusions and recesses. As the largest surface area in
any room, walls play a substantial role in establishing a

CHAPTER 6
WALLS

bold or subtle color scheme, and in creating the basic mood
for the furnishings that are to be placed within the room.
Walls must therefore be carefully used to express the decorating approach; they should never be ignored or treated
only as a peripheral element. How they are colored and embellished can often make the difference between success and
failure in the fulfillment of an interior-design project.

The options for wall decoration are overwhelming: paint,
paneling, patterned wallpaper, textured wall coverings, mirror, fabric, combinations of two or more of these materials.
The early colonists had none of these choices available to
them, and at first had to be content with whatever enrichment their building materials—wood planking and beams,
logs, or bricks—provided as an interior as well as exterior
surface. Later, when they learned how to brew colors out of
plants and flowers, they applied these hues or simple white-
washes to interior walls over coats of plaster. Structural
beams provided additional ornamentation, and the more in-
ventive colonists taught themselves to decorate their walls
with patterns set by stencils, applied sometimes in allover
fashion, sometimes merely for border decoration. Itinerant
artists, skilled in stenciling, could be hired for modest fees
by the less handy settlers.

Hand-printed wallpaper came into popular use among the
wealthy Americans of the mid-eighteenth century, who im-

Walls painted in a dark sepia-toned enamel dramatize beautiful white mantel and woodwork, enhancing a mood of restrained elegance.

Painted paneling and stenciled walls re-create the look of a Colonial bedroom. Stencil pattern was inspired by the print of the quilted coverlet.

ported the latest designs from France, England, and the Orient. Today in some of America's proudest restorations, we can see examples of the magnificent floral, geometric, and architectural motifs of this early wallpaper as well as exquisitely rendered murals depicting panoramic scenes.

Paint nowadays is not only within the price range of virtually everyone; it is manufactured in an unlimited array of hues and tints, and in finishes that range from flat and semigloss to high lacquers that rival the reflective sheen of mirror glass. Paint is made as an oil- or water-based product, and either type of paint offers certain pluses and minuses. Oil paint fills a room with fumes when first applied, and it is "dirtier" to work with (its stains are harder to remove from hands, clothing, and other spattered surfaces), but it is

Small-scale floral wall-paper, embellished by pink molding, is consistent with the highly decorative style of this formal sitting room.

extremely hardy. It is therefore a good choice for rooms that get heavy use and where walls need frequent scrubbing. Water-based (latex) paints have almost no smell, can be applied easily with rollers by do-it-yourselfers, but are somewhat less durable than oil-based paints if surfaces require frequent spot washing or scrubbing.

Wallpaper is now mass-produced in a mind-boggling choice of patterns and color combinations. Those manufactured on the more efficient and lower-cost roller principle are often styled in colors and designs on a par with the most exquisite (and far more expensive) screen prints.

VARIETY OF POSSIBLE WALL TREATMENTS

- paint
- paper, textured or print
- paneling
- fabric
- mirror
- applied architectural elements

With so much to choose from, how does one decide whether paint, wallpaper, paneling, fabric, or any other of the available options is the right answer for a specific room? Often two or more possibilities are viable for the appearance of the same room; but there are other critical factors besides aesthetic preference that can determine the decision.

The first consideration should be the physical condition of the walls. If they are badly cracked, blemished, or discolored, they will probably require the kind of sheathing that totally "repairs" a wall visually—such as paneling, mirror, shirred fabric, or a well-lined wall covering that is thickly textured.

If the walls are to be used to provide a dark and dramatic backdrop, or as a delicately tinted surface for a personal collection of art, then paint would be the preferable material—a deep and highly lacquered texture for the first situation, a flat-finished and softly colored shade for the second.

The walls may be in good condition but actually lacking in any architectural enrichment, a sore point for a family who wish to extend the period flavor of their furniture into a room's backgrounds. In this instance the addition of molding, a fireplace or fireplace mantel, documentary or architectural wallpaper, and beams or bricks that serve a purely decorative role offer viable solutions.

If a room is of an unfortunate size—either too large or too small—then the wall treatment can help to make it seem more intimate or more spacious. Paint, the least expensive of wall-decorating materials, is often the most effective in achieving these ends. Dark and bold colors tend to make the walls of a room close in, and therefore diminish the barny feeling of an oversize interior. Pale and soft colors, and especially white, will open up space in a room that needs its walls "pushed out" to visually enlarge its size.

Wall color can also alter the visual dimensions of a room. By putting a deeper or bolder tone on the short walls of a long, narrow room, you can make its space appear wider or squarer. A pale tint will visually heighten a ceiling (the fifth wall of a room), while a dark color will lower it.

Paint can magically wipe out eyesores such as old-fash-

Laminated silk wall covering is a perfect background for a handsome and unusual dining room that blends Chippendale and contemporary furniture, and serves to "frame" a collection of paintings.

ioned radiators, awkward beams and jogs, or a poorly designed mantel. This you can accomplish simply by painting everything—walls, eyesores, woodwork—in the same shade, one strong or bold enough to make all blemishes blend into one wash of color.

Conversely, handsome molding, mantels, window reveals, and other architectural jewels can be enhanced by the application of a paint that contrasts dramatically with the color applied to the walls.

Wall treatment can also bring out the period flavor of traditional furnishings, or it can endow them with contempo-

Tall and magnificent coromandel screen punctuates a small comfortable seating arrangement in one corner of a large living room.

rary flair. Merely by changing the wall color from an authentic Federal or Colonial hue to a bold and sizzling tone not associated with traditional wall decoration, one can immediately "update" the mood, investing traditional furniture with a fresh and vibrant new look. Altogether, paint is a relatively inexpensive yet extremely effective way of changing a family's approach within the broad alternatives of American Traditional decorating when they have reached the point where they want to live with a different style or mood.

Wall paint can also create "the space that isn't there." A contrasting wall color gives the illusion of an entry in a foyerless living room, or makes a dining alcove or dressing area seem more important and dramatic than it really is.

It's fine to collect paint chips when you're trying to narrow down your color alternatives—but never make a decision on wall paint keyed to a tiny sample of color. Buy a pint of whatever hue you are considering, and try it out on the wall to get a much more realistic idea of how it will "read" as a larger expanse. The same also applies to wallpaper, which looks very different in the hand or in a showroom, as a small sample, from the way it does when it completely blankets a wall. Tape up a large sample to your wall before buying the rolls you'll need.

Wall coverings—which include paper with printed patterns, as well as those textural effects which emulate all kinds of natural materials—come second to paint as a viable option for walls. If you want the walls to carry the lion's share of a room's pattern, then printed wallpaper is your choice. Many professionals like to use a wall-covering pattern in concert with a matching print in the drapery fabric, or one that is reiterated as sofa and chair covers. You'll find that many manufacturers offer correlated collections of fabrics and wallpapers which contain different but related designs, all available in the same choice of compatible colors. These collections make it possible to use a wall covering of one design (such as a small-scale print) with a fabric pattern of much bolder dimensions, though similar in style and identical in color execution. These coordinates can guarantee the success of a pattern-with-pattern approach to room decoration.

Textured wall coverings produce an interesting surface without the constrictions of pattern. Paper-backed or laminated silk, burlap, linen, grass cloth, suede, and other leather-like textures, as well as wood grains, are among the most popular of such textural effects. These heavy wall coverings are especially efficient in "restoring" blemished walls, and they make an excellent choice for a small room where some kind of textural interest is needed. They can also be used with equal success in large rooms, though they do tend to run up the budget when large quantities are needed.

Avoid using bold wallpapers in living areas, where they can become tiresome, or in a bedroom, where a certain degree of serenity is required.

The new strippable wallpapers make it easy to do the job yourself, without the extra expense of installation. Strippable wall coverings can also be removed very easily, when a change of treatment is desired.

Most wall-covering manufacturers use protective coatings or heavy vinyl surfaces for their products, so that they are all but impervious to dirt and staining. A little washing with soap and water, and presto, the dirt or stains wipe away. Be sure to limit yourself to these kinds of wall coverings in heavy-duty areas such as bathrooms and kitchens. Such surface protection also ensures a longer life for wall coverings that you choose for dining rooms, family rooms, and bedrooms.

In recent years, fabric-covered walls have become popular for professionally decorated rooms. Fabric offers a rich but subtle sense of texture, and when it is shirred the walls take on a highly decorative look. Fabric can be shirred from rods that are installed from crown to baseboard molding and can easily be removed for laundering or cleaning. Such shirred walls are therefore not at all impractical, as many people assume; in fact, they are often chosen by designers to cover marred walls, since no preparation (as would be necessary

Mirrored screens add sparkle and a sense of space to a small dining alcove in an apartment.

before the application of paint or wallpaper) is required.

What often makes a den, library, or informal family room especially cozy and inviting is the rich and warm wood graining of paneled walls. This is why paneling is still a favorite way to decorate backgrounds, especially today, when laminated veneers on plywood, so much more reasonable than solid paneling, are available in all kinds of woods and finishes. These modern paneling materials are a far cry in terms of cost from the exquisite boiseries and splendid paneling that we associate with the grand interiors of affluent eighteenth- and nineteenth-century homes. As a matter of fact, they are often just as effective. And if you want to spend even less, you can choose from a multitude of wood-look thermoset plastic panelings that are hard to distinguish from the real thing.

Paneling comes in almost as many grainings and shades of wood as there are available in nature. Avoid dark grainings for rooms that get very little natural light, and do not choose too elegant a texture for a setting filled with American country pieces. Barn siding, for example, works nicely for an interior styled with Chippendale reproductions. As with everything else, there must be a sensible correlation of color, material, and style of wall covering to furnishings.

Paneling should be installed by a professional unless you are extremely handy at this sort of thing. Many paneling manufacturers (and producers of wall coverings, too) offer excellent instructions for doing it yourself; but such projects are not worth attempting unless you are sure of your ability to handle them well.

There are many other wall embellishments available that can solve both decorative and functional requirements. Mirror, while expensive, is enormously rewarding as a space expander; visually it doubles the size of any area where it is used, while adding the dividends of sparkle and light. Applied molding can give a boxy high-rise apartment the detail necessary to relate backgrounds to furnishings with a strong period flavor. Antique or exquisite copies of American Traditional mantels can also dramatize the period style of a room, and establish a focal point around which the furniture can be grouped. And the lightweight polystyrene beams that look so amazingly like the old wood structural supports in a Colonial house, and are easy to apply, can convert an ordinary living or dining room into a warm and richly endowed eighteenth-century interior.

More than one wall covering can be used in the same room, but such mixing can be tricky and is often best left to the guidance of a professional. Applied molding can be added to wallpapered or painted walls; the space below a chair rail can be fabric-covered; the wall space above the molding can be painted in a coordinate color, or vice versa; and a bed wall can be shirred with fabric while the other walls are painted in one of the major colors of the fabric print. If price is an object, panel only one wall of a den or family room, or mirror just one short wall in your dining room. You can obviate the need for hanging paintings by sheathing your walls with a personal collection of wonderful old outsize quilts.

You should not get carried away by the many options for wall decoration. You'll want to make your walls play a stellar role, if that is the way the decorating plan works best, but you should explore only those possibilities which are really compatible with your other ideas and goals. Let your walls work to whatever degree is most desirable, and you will be surprised at how much they can enhance the final result—dramatically or subtly, whichever is your aim.

Simple tie-back draperies frame a bay window of a country American sitting area.

Window decoration—
or window treatment, as it is usually called—is unquestion-
ably one of the most creative facets of interior design. But
window treatments are never finishing touches or the final

CHAPTER 7
WINDOW TREATMENTS

accent that makes a room come together. Because they are
an integral part of any design plan, and play a functional as
well as a decorative role, windows must be dealt with during the preliminary stages of a decorating project. Along
with walls, floors, color schemes, and major furnishings,
window treatments must be factored into those early tenta-
tive decisions and the final blueprint that evolves from
them.

Seventeenth-century houses were the first buildings in
America to have windows constructed of glass, a material
that had to be imported and was, therefore, expensive. The
typical small window of such an early New England house
had diamond-shaped panes set in lead strips in a casement
design reminiscent of Elizabethan architecture. Some of the
windows included both stationary and casement panels.

The production of glass in this country in the eighteenth
century made the material cheaper and more readily available. The new style of window that emerged at this time
was the double-hung sash variety with mullioned panes—
this due to the fact that glass was still manufactured in
small sizes only. Later, in the early nineteenth century, when
panes were made longer and wider, fewer mullions were
needed. Still larger panes of glass were used for the stick-

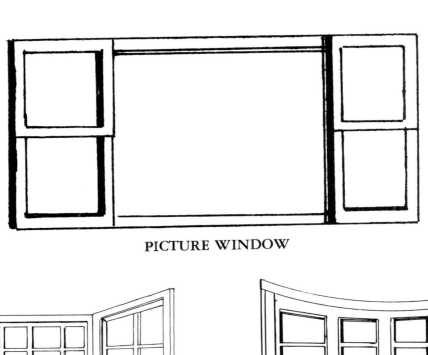

PICTURE WINDOW

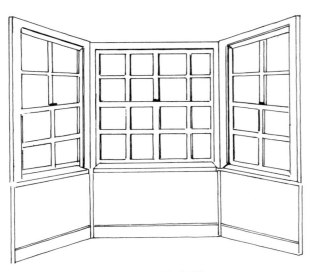

BAY WINDOW

BOW WINDOW

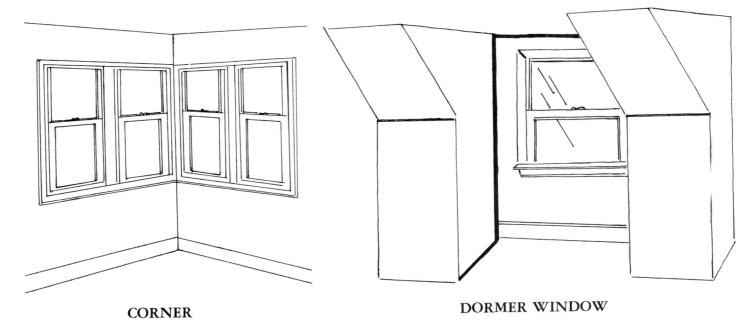

CORNER

DORMER WINDOW

AMERICAN TRADITIONAL

defeat the window's major purpose and obscure the beautiful scenery. In order to provide ventilation through the side sections, your treatment may have to be pulled back so far that the window will appear to be out of proportion. This can be a real problem when there is a radiator or air conditioner beneath the center pane. Your treatment should correct the misproportions while camouflaging the radiator or air conditioner, or even perhaps an unattractive view.

BAY AND BOW WINDOWS. A bay window has three or more windows set at an angle to each other in a recessed area. A bow window is always curved. There are many varieties within each style. For example, either kind of window could have a window seat, or glass panes that extend to the floor. Whichever one you're lucky enough to possess, use some imagination and make the most of its decorative potential, while still relating it to the style of the room and the design of the furnishings.

CORNER WINDOWS are two windows of any style that meet at a corner of the room. Because they offer two light exposures and two views with no space for the treatment in between, they can be difficult to handle. The answer is to deal with them as one unit, rather than two windows. With this approach you will not be sacrificing the view or any of your light source.

DORMER WINDOWS, often found in eighteenth-century-style houses, are small and deeply recessed into a gable, an alcove-like extension from the roof of the house. Because the gable may be very narrow, you can run into the problem of having no wall space on which to apply your treatment. This is usually solved with shades, blinds, shutters, or curtains installed within the window casing.

AWNING WINDOWS are made up of horizontal glass panes that can be opened at an angle. Styles of awning windows range from one panel to many panels. Since the panes can be adjusted to any angle, these windows offer good draft-free ventilation (especially in tropical areas, where they keep out the rain as well). A jalousie is a style of awning window that contains a multitude of narrow panes. Ventilation is a primary purpose of jalousies, so treat them simply. Also remember to allow for clearance for the crank that opens them.

FRENCH DOORS are really window doors. They can be made up of a single door, though usually they work as a pair. In planning your treatment, choose one that allows for easy passage. As with casements, if the French doors are out-swinging, you won't be as limited in your treatment choices. Should the doors swing in, it would be best either to attach the treatment directly to the doors, using rods that swing open when the doors do, or to frame the window with a treatment such as a cornice or lambrequin.

SLIDING GLASS DOORS can be part of the solid wall construction or part of a whole wall of glass. Either way, your treatment should permit passage through the doorway. Your main concern with window walls (with or without doors) will be to protect the room from too much summer sun or winter cold, and to ensure access to an attractive view. You'll also want to soften the black expanse of glass that emerges at night (unless you are fortunate enough to have a night view as well).

RANCH WINDOWS are wide, shallow, and placed high on the wall. They are usually found in contemporary homes, especially in those ranch-style houses built in the 1950s. Because of their high position, they often seem to be out of proportion to the rest of the room. For this reason, it's usually best to give them a simple treatment, one that makes them blend into the background.

CLERESTORY WINDOWS are shallow strips placed along and just below the ceiling. They provide privacy while admitting

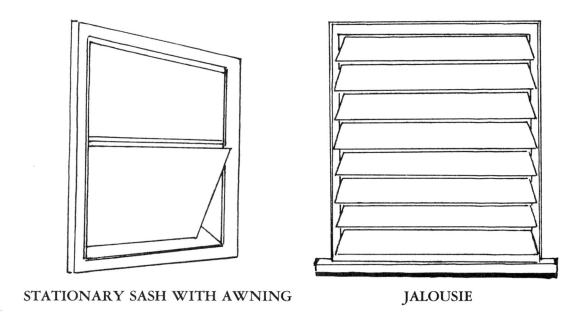

STATIONARY SASH WITH AWNING

JALOUSIE

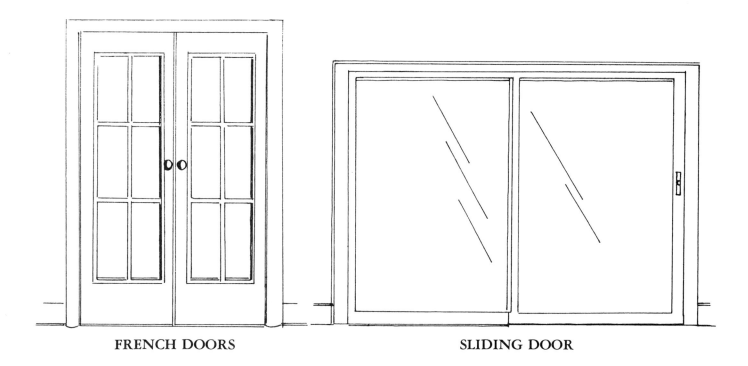

FRENCH DOORS

SLIDING DOOR

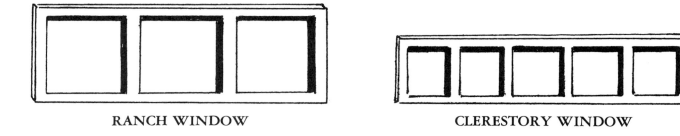

RANCH WINDOW

CLERESTORY WINDOW

CATHEDRAL WINDOW

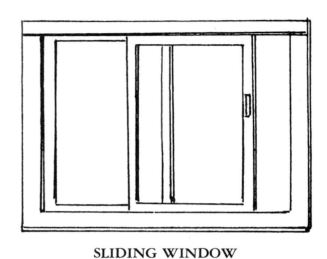

SLIDING WINDOW

light and air. Leave them unadorned, or if light control is necessary, cover them as you would ranch windows. Should they follow the shape of a pitched ceiling, you might choose a custom-designed shade or venetian blind.

CATHEDRAL WINDOWS follow the pitch of a cathedral-shaped ceiling. The entire window is often large, consisting of a window wall below and a pitched window above. You can treat just the lower portion, leaving the pitched area at the top open, or you can decorate both areas. Simplicity should be your guideline in dealing with this special kind of window.

HORIZONTALLY SLIDING WINDOWS are almost like double-hung windows placed on their sides, though one pane is often fixed and only the other is movable. A wide variety of treatments will work with these windows.

ARCHED WINDOWS have a curved top and usually go all the way to the floor. Although they are most often found in

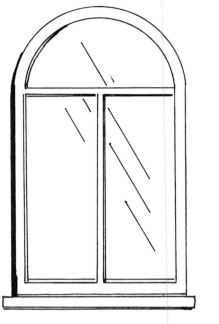

ARCHED WINDOW

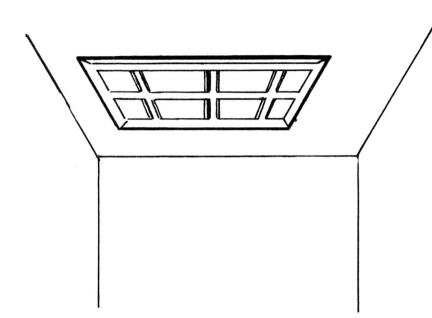

SKYLIGHT

older homes and are considered "traditional" in feeling, they consort well with modern furnishings. This is an attractive style that can enhance your room's architectural interest, so you'll want to select a treatment that will emphasize the windows. Sometimes French doors are designed in this form.

SKYLIGHTS are windows set into the roof itself, and can be left uncovered so that as much natural light as possible will filter in. Occasionally, however, it may be desirable to subdue the light and glare. The best solutions are those which can be installed against the glass and which can be controlled easily from below. Shades and venetian blinds mounted with special hardware are both good solutions.

THE PRIMARY FUNCTION OF WINDOWS

The most obvious function of windows, as was said earlier, is to admit light and air into our homes. However, we rarely let windows provide as much light as is possible;

often we want to limit, to varying degrees, the amount of light that enters during the day. How much light control is needed depends on the exposure of the room—the compass direction in which the windows face. A northern exposure gets little or no direct sunlight; an eastern one receives a flood of morning sun; and a western exposure gets the strong sunlight of the afternoon. These three require less control than the southern exposure, where sunlight may create too much heat and light during certain hours of the day. Such an overdose of heat and light can fade fabrics, wilt plants, and result in higher electricity bills due to increased use of air conditioning.

At one window you may want a variety of controls. This can best be accomplished with a combination of two or more kinds of window treatment. For example, you might combine lined draperies in a heavy fabric—totally cutting off all light when drawn—with glass curtains to filter light. Of course, both of these could be opened for full exposure, giving you three degrees of light control. And there are still other options which we will discuss later in this chapter when we describe window-treatment design.

Windows must also provide ventilation, and whatever treatment is chosen must not interfere with this other very essential role. Assess your choice of possible window treatments in terms of how well they will hold up to blowing breezes and dust, should you plan to open your windows frequently. This concern is particularly important if you live in a city. Dark colors or fabrics that can be easily cleaned or laundered are your best choices here.

Window treatments also control temperature. While most homes are equipped with air conditioning, this is not always enough to fight off a summer heat wave. During winter cold snaps we can also suffer as heat escapes from our homes. Specific kinds of window treatments are helpful in each instance. Lined draperies in a heavy fabric can block out the heat of a blazing summer sun during the day. Or you might want to use translucent shade cloth designed to filter light so that enough comes through to keep a room cheerful and plants healthy, but without some of the sun's heat. Another alternative might be venetian blinds, chosen in a shiny aluminum finish so that the surface reflects away about half of the sunlight; their slats can be adjusted easily, permitting a great degree of flexibility in the control of light.

Window treatments also provide control over privacy, so that the neighbors or passersby cannot peer into your home at will. Daytime worries are usually minimal, especially when it is brighter outside the house than indoors. When windows are exposed to public view, however, some kind of privacy control, such as sheer curtains, or those woven of casement cloth, might be advisable.

Interior lighting presents an even bigger privacy problem at night, especially if part of the window needs to be kept open for ventilation. Usually people prefer to block out a good part of a large window because of the ominous expanse of black that would dominate the room at night. The window treatments for such rooms must be designed to accommodate these problems.

If you have an attractive view, then you will want a window treatment that will let you enjoy it, usually one simple enough so that attention is not distracted from the outdoors, be it a beautiful garden or a city panorama at night.

Windows can be dramatized as important architectural and/or design elements in your interiors, or they can be made almost to disappear by blending into the background. When treated as significant design features, they can sustain a period style; add texture, pattern, and color; or provide an undistinguished setting with architectural embellishment.

If your windows do have architectural interest in the form of attractive molding, emphasize this by leaving the molding exposed and placing the treatment within the case, or by painting the molding a color that contrasts with the walls.

Whatever mood or style you decide on for your room, carry it through with your window treatments. While you can use your treatment to accentuate a pure eighteenth-century look or to support a more eclectic approach, there should be some consistency as to degree of elegance or informality. In other words, your window treatment should help carry through a mood of elegance and formality established in the furnishings. You would not choose a satiny damask and a treatment that uses tassels and fringes for a rustic country living room any more than you would select a coarsely woven cotton for a formal Chippendale dining room.

Window treatments, as we have said, can also serve to camouflage an awkward window—one that is out of scale with the room or poorly positioned. Two ways to do this—in effect making the window disappear by blending it with the walls—are to paint louvered shutters in the same color as the wall, and to use draperies in a fabric that matches the wall paint.

Many patterned wallpapers are offered with matching fabric, so using the same pattern at walls and windows is still another way of blending in the window or making it appear less important or obvious.

Window treatments can also hide radiators or air conditioners, or block out unsightly views such as a fire escape. They can also provide sound and temperature insulation. These problems or needs should all be taken into consideration when the window treatment is being planned.

VARIETY OF WINDOW TREATMENTS

It is not necessary to duplicate the design of an eighteenth-century window treatment to create the overall mood of an American Traditional room, but it was during this period of our history that beautiful window dressing flourished, and many of the ways we decorate our windows today have been shaped by those earlier styles.

Such relatively elaborate window treatments are seen in the more elegant eighteenth-century houses in Virginia, the Carolinas, Washington's Georgetown section, and Georgia. Draperies were tied back not just once, but often twice, and were fashioned from luxurious silks and damasks. Swagged valances and decoratively shaped, fabric-covered cornices topped these draperies, which were often trimmed with fringe or gimp. Decorative tassels also came into play on both tiebacks and swagged valances. Swags and jabots were used alone or with additional curtaining.

Decorative rosettes were favored as bold accents to hold back the draperies, and on occasion window hangings were supported by rods finished with decorative finials. Simple curtains, hung straight and set within the reveals, were, of course, more popular for humbler houses and interiors. These, and the very elegant and dramatically embellished draperies and valances of the more affluent colonists, continue to influence the way we design our window treatments today.

DRAPERIES AND CURTAINS

Since the eighteenth century, draperies and curtains have become the most popular and versatile of window treatments. They can be employed for almost any kind of window, and can be used together or in combination with other options such as shades, shutters, and blinds.

Draperies are usually made of medium- to heavyweight fabric and hung in folds or pleats from rods or poles. They can be made full enough to cover the entire window when hung on traverse rods, then pulled back to serve as side panels, or they may be used over curtains as added ornamentation, pulled back, or hung straight. The kind of fabric chosen—damask or brocade, as opposed to cotton or linen—and the amount of gimp, tassel, and fringe utilized will determine the degree of formality of the drapery treatment. When lined and interlined, draperies help to insulate a room against cold and noise.

Sheer curtains, sometimes referred to as glass curtains, are almost always used in concert with draperies, whether as stationary panels or pulled across the entire window. When covering a large expanse such as a picture window, they can also be hung from traverse rods, filtering the sharp sunlight

Roman shades plus matching tie-back curtains decorate high-set window in a family living room.

A combination of valance, stationary drapery panels, and matchstick blinds integrates two separate windows with deep reveals.

but letting sufficient light brighten the room during daytime hours. The translucency of the sheer or casement cloth permits sufficient light to come through while also providing needed privacy.

In addition to these sheer full-length curtains employed in tandem with draperies, many other styles and kinds of curtains are favored for different modes of window treatment. One of the most popular is café curtains, which can be made of any fabric—sheer, patterned, printed—and hung singly or in tiers. "Cafés" are suspended from rods and are usually opened and closed by hand; when they are installed in tiers, the lower panels serve the cause of privacy and the top panel is used to control the amount of light and ventilation that enters the room.

Café curtains, as well as other short- and long-style curtains (cafés do not usually hang longer than the sill) are de-

Wood shutters shirred with fabric are a simple solution to this pretty Palladian window.

Draperies made with a "header" that is shirred on a wooden pole or rod are a simple and very popular way of treating a window and making it seem larger.

signed with numerous headings. They can be shirred or gathered on poles or can be pleated or scalloped and held to a pole by rings. Pinch pleats or box pleats can also be used as headings for curtains and draperies. Another popular choice is the ruffled curtain, an informal style with ruffled edges and hems and usually endowed with ruffled tieback and valances for a very delightful feminine look.

WINDOW SHADES

Window shades were once considered the last resort in window dressing; today they are often a first choice. This is because shades now come in an extraordinarily wide range of colors and textures and are remarkably versatile; they can be laminated with a fabric matching another used elsewhere in the room (or the coordinating draperies), they can be decoratively stenciled or hand-painted, and they can be embellished with tapes, fringes, and appliqués. They work beautifully in partnership with draperies, in place of curtains. If installed reverse-roll, they need not be covered by a cornice; otherwise, by some kind of valance or perhaps a tailored lambrequin.

Because window shades are so simple and tailored, even when used with a trim lambrequin, they are often a perfect choice for a small or cluttered room. And if you are handy, you can do the laminating or decorating yourself, using stencils or fabric cutouts for appliqués, or simply painting freehand, if you have the talent. Many of the adhesive-coated shades available for laminating come with easy-to-follow instructions.

In addition to this basic roll-up variety of shade, there are decorative Roman and Austrian styles which pull up on tapes. Roman shades form pleats of fabric when the shade is raised. The fabric chosen should be just heavy enough so that the shade falls into strong horizontal pleats when

Striped draperies are imaginatively tacked back to reveal the contrast of a white lining.

Balloon shades, fashionable for all kinds of rooms, are full and billowy when the shade is raised, flat when lowered.

pulled up. Roman shades are obviously more formal than the roll-up kind and can be utilized quite differently. Two or more small windows can be integrated by one large roll-up shade, while a wide contemporary window wall, treated with a series of several matching Roman shades, will work well with an interior filled with formal and traditional furnishings.

Austrian shades work much the same way that Roman shades do, but they pull up into a very decorative shirred effect with a scalloped lower edge. They are especially compatible with formal period settings. It is suggested that you have a professional make either Roman or Austrian shades.

For informality, the roll-up bamboo style of shade has become extremely popular in recent years, thanks to its low cost and wide versatility. These shades diffuse light and provide subtle textural accent. Even more popular are the much lighter-weight matchstick blinds which serve a similar role but can be used with draperies or overcurtains in the place of sheer or casement curtains.

Bottom-up shades offer still another option. They pull up from the bottom of the window or the floor and can be used the way café curtains are—to block out unattractive views, or to hide an air conditioner that is not in use. They are perfect for ground-floor windows where privacy is a critical concern.

As we mentioned in the case of Roman shades, a series of shades can be more effective than one large shade. And for those windows where you have hung your drapery from rods mounted near the ceiling, try installing your window shades at the ceiling too, rather than at the tip of the window. This will give you one clean, unbroken line that adds a sense of height to your window.

For unusual windows—clerestory, skylight, or cathedral, for instance—special shades can be ordered.

BLINDS AND SHUTTERS

Venetian blinds are made of adjustable horizontal slats of wood or metal. They offer a wide degree of control of light

The large window wall of contemporary apartments can be screened by vertical blinds which offer excellent light control and blend easily with a variety of style moods.

and airflow, especially with the narrower slats featured in today's most popular styles. Venetian blinds are offered in just about any color or finish possible, from shiny metallic to flat. Since they afford an enormous range in degree of light control and can be chosen in colors that blend in with the background, they are often preferred for small rooms, or areas in which it is desirable to play down the background and windows rather than dramatize them. These blinds can, of course, be used in conjunction with draperies.

Vertical blinds are similar in structure to venetian blinds, but here the slats run vertically instead of horizontally and are usually much wider. Vertical blinds offer many degrees of light and air control and can be ordered in a variety of colors and textures. Because they can be attached to ceiling tracks and thus extend to the floor, they work beautifully in covering an entire window wall, or camouflaging two badly misproportioned windows or awkwardly placed corner windows.

The most stable installation for vertical blinds is a track on the sill or floor in addition to the one on the ceiling, but sometimes this is impractical and a chain running through the bottom of the panels can be used instead. Vertical blinds are obviously a modern concept, but could be used in American Traditional rooms that were styled with a freewheeling eclectic approach.

Shutters have been with us since the colonists first used them to trim the exterior of their windows; they are often popular choices inside a house as well, offering a rich, warm, and architecturally important way to handle window treatment. Shutters are generally made of wood, but metal is also employed, though much less frequently. Shutters are extremely versatile because while they are a traditional outside window treatment, they also work beautifully in certain kinds of eclectic and contemporary interiors. Shutters feature movable louvers which can be adjusted to admit varying degrees of light and air. They come now in a wide choice of styles as well, running from the more conventional solid wood panels or louvers to wood frames that support gathered or stretched inserts of plain, textured, or patterned fabrics. If used in sets and installed in tiers, these framed shutters function in a manner similar to that of café curtains, with the bottom set closed for privacy and the top shutters opened for light and ventilation. Because they add architectural enrichment to any room, they are handsome enough used alone, but they also mix with other window embellishments, such as undercurtains, shades, and draperies. Shutters are usually hinged to the window frame and fit within the window.

CORNICES AND VALANCES

The simple swag and jabot—a width of fabric draped across the top of a window, with the extra yardage falling down in so-called "jabot" panels—were often a favorite look in country-style and more formal Colonial houses. Window-treatment toppings of this kind, especially upholstered cornices or softly draped valances, are still popular.

Cornices are usually made of plywood or some other stiff material such as buckram. They can be purchased in this raw state in department or home-center stores, then painted or covered in fabric, mirror, or almost any other material. Cornices usually extend from the ceiling to several inches

Upholstered cornice and matching draperies lend architectural importance to what would otherwise be an ordinary and seemingly undersized window.

below the top of the curtains or draperies, and they help to dramatize the window treatment as well as to provide it with a more finished and architecturally important look.

In much the same role as cornices, valances cover up drapery heading and hardware, but provide a much softer and

Decoratively shaped valance and matching draperies soften the modern architecture of a comfortable country-style living room. Sheer curtains conceal only the lower half of the windows, admitting ample light.

sometimes more elegant appearance, especially if the fabric is fringed or tape-trimmed. Valances are most often made of the same fabric used for the draperies, and are either pleated or swagged. To soften the hard-edged look of cornices, one can have them cut into patterns of symmetrical curves.

We talked earlier of lambrequins as a possible choice for use with French doors. Lambrequins are actually an extended version of the cornice; they not only cover the top of the windows, but frame the sides down to the sill or the floor. They also can be shaped, and covered in fabric or painted, as with cornices, to match the curtains or the woodwork.

A collection of plants on table and floor and suspended from ceiling composes the daytime window treatment of this room. At night, the window shade, which matches side draperies, is lowered.

OTHER WINDOW CHOICES

We have now covered the major viable window-treatment possibilities. But there are also other options, though ones not so familiar or so popular as those described above. As a rule, it is not wise to go for a faddish or way-out approach in designing windows for an American Traditional room, even one with a freewheeling eclectic mood; but sometimes, in a limited instance, a professional will create a window dressing that is a bit audacious but can work.

The balloon shade, which has gained sudden and extensive popularity in recent seasons, is a pull-up shade distinguished by segments that are extremely full and billowy when the shade is raised. It is very decorative, but not always the best choice for a small room, as it eats up space visually.

Sliding panels are also occasionally added for window dressing. These are made up of vertically hung rectangular panels which move along a ceiling track. They can be fashioned of any hard material, from acrylic plastic to perforated hardboard. Shoji and fretwork panels are two of the more elegant expressions of this approach. Freestanding panels, such as decorative screens, can also be employed—usually as a pair placed at either side to frame and dramatize the window.

In choosing fabrics for a specific window treatment, make sure that they are part of the total fabric plan for the room, not some unconnected pattern brought in on a whim. It usually makes sense to repeat at the window some texture or pattern used on upholstery; this integrates the design of the room. If a pattern is used, for example, for a sofa and/or chairs placed on one side of the room, it should be repeated somewhere on the other side for balance.

Obviously, many factors besides aesthetic preference will shape your final decisions on window dressing. We have mentioned some earlier: privacy, light and air control, insulation, camouflage, fade and soil resistance, ease of maintenance. Putting all these requirements on paper will help you come down to the kind of window design that will work best for each room of your house.

HOW TO BUY CURTAINS AND DRAPERIES

Curtains and draperies, the most popular window-treatment style for traditional interiors, can be fashioned in one of three ways: 1) ready-made, 2) made-to-measure, and 3) custom-made.

Ready-mades, as the name indicates, can be purchased and

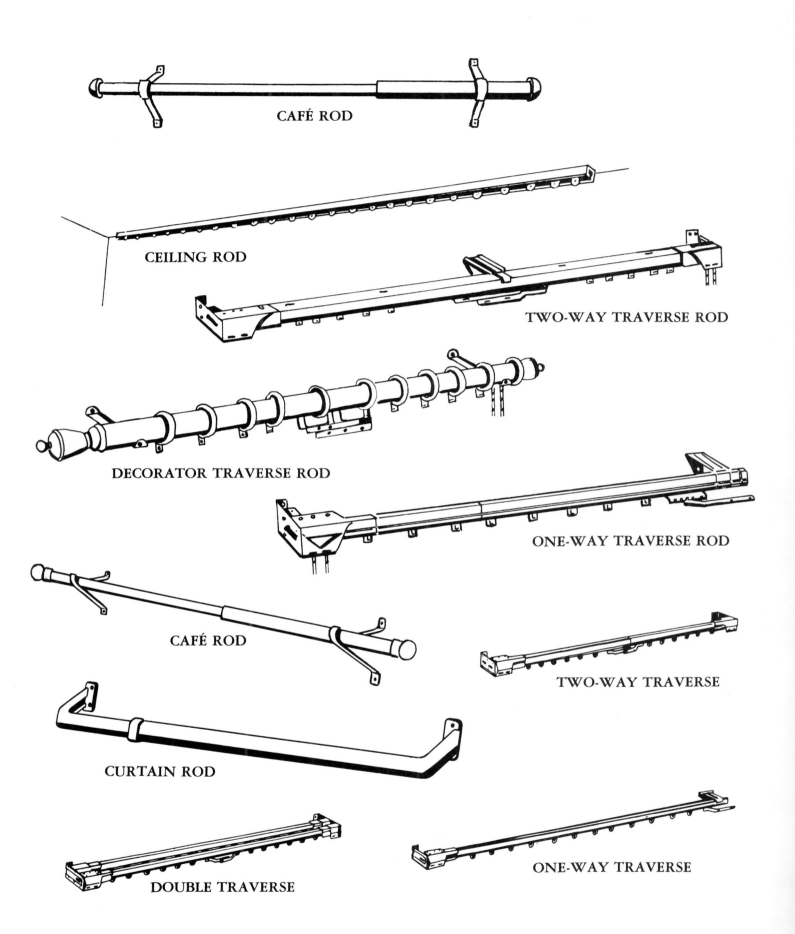

CAFÉ ROD

CEILING ROD

TWO-WAY TRAVERSE ROD

DECORATOR TRAVERSE ROD

ONE-WAY TRAVERSE ROD

CAFÉ ROD

TWO-WAY TRAVERSE

CURTAIN ROD

DOUBLE TRAVERSE

ONE-WAY TRAVERSE

AMERICAN TRADITIONAL

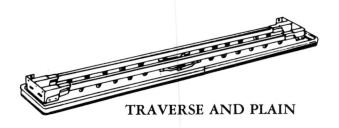

TRAVERSE AND PLAIN

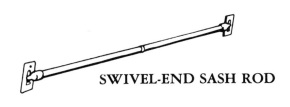

SWIVEL-END SASH ROD

SINGLE CURTAIN ROD

SPRING-TENSION ROD

SASH ROD

DRAPERY CRANE

SLIP-ON HOOK

**CAFÉ ROD WITH ARM
SUPPORTS AND RINGS**

**CAFÉ ROD
WITH SUPPORT**

**PLEATER HOOK
WITH RING**

PLEATER HOOK

**CLIP-ON
CAFÉ RING**

**POINTED
PIN-ON HOOK**

**ROUND
PIN-ON HOOK**

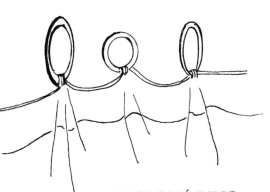

EYELET CAFÉ RING

hung immediately—no need for hemming or special ordering. You can choose from fully made-up designs, kept in stock in drapery stores or drapery departments of stores that carry furniture and home furnishings. These are usually offered in a number of standard lengths and widths, and in a wide variety of fabric patterns, prints, and textures. The big benefits are lower prices and same-day service, though obviously the choices are not unlimited.

Many stores offer made-to-measure drapery service, something of a middle alternative between ready-mades and custom-mades. For the best results, take careful measurements of your windows, and go to a store offering made-to-measures in a wide choice of fabrics. The store will then have a drapery manufacturer execute your order. Here you will have a wider choice of fabric and style possibilities than with ready-mades, and you will get draperies that will fit your specific window measurements. The price will depend upon fabric choice and the size and style of the window treatment. You will often have to wait many weeks for the order to be completed and delivered.

Custom-made draperies offer the widest possible choice in fabric and style. You can have just about any kind of treatment made and in almost any fabric available, and you will have the benefit of a custom drapery workroom whose quality of workmanship and design will be high—but so will be the prices, naturally. You will also enjoy certain conveniences when buying custom-mades. A workroom or store representative will measure your windows himself, and can knowledgeably discuss all style possibilities. When the draperies or curtains are ready, someone will be sent to your house to install the hardware and hang the treatment.

A word should also be said here about linings and hardware. Linings protect fabrics from sun-fading and present a uniform look from the outside of the house. Lined draperies will hang in richer folds, and the room will be better insulated against summer sun and winter winds. Some of the drapery linings that can be used have added features that insulate, repel rain, and absorb sound.

Installation of hardware is another important aspect of window treatment. The style of your window design will determine the kind of hardware needed, and your store will help you make the right choices, but there are a few basics you should understand.

The best kind of hardware for draperies is the traverse rod. It is adjustable and can be installed on the ceiling, wall, or window casing. Through the use of a cord, a pulley, and plastic glides, it allows you to open and close draperies easily with two panels that meet in the center (two-way draw) or a single panel that moves to one side (one-way draw). The rod shows only when the drapery is open.

There are many other special rods and combinations, such as double rods to hold heavy draperies and sheer curtains on the same piece of hardware. For other kinds of necessary hardware, such as hinges for shutters or decorative poles for curtains hung from loops, talk to the store that is supplying you with the window treatment to ascertain exactly what kind of hardware you should buy and how much you'll need.

What furniture designs are to be chosen, and where they are to be placed, are two of the most critical decisions affecting the decoration of any room. Saying that, however, we have put the cart be-

CHAPTER 8
FURNITURE CHOICE AND ARRANGEMENT

fore the horse: before we know what to purchase, we must first have a floor plan—a blueprint that nails down each and every furniture piece required to complete the room. It is only after this blueprint has been established that you can begin your search for the necessary pieces—a search that must itself be as deliberate as the mapping out of your floor-plan strategy. Furniture is costly; it cannot be replaced every season if it should break down, start to look seedy, or simply prove a grand mistake. Your investment will be too large to let this happen.

Furniture is functional as well as decorative, whereas many other design elements in an interior—wallpaper, accessories, paintings, and so on—serve no other role except to enhance and embellish. We sit, sleep, rest, dine, and watch television using furniture. Furniture is indispensable to our comfort in every way. It also serves the equally significant purpose of storage. Furniture organizes our linens, silver, glassware, personal possessions, and clothing. Furniture holds books and all sorts of electronic equipment, and it supports the necessary lamps and accessories that are spaced

U-shaped arrangement of modular sectional sofas provides optimum seating around a modern hearth.

ture, you should think twice about buying a bold graphic.

Finally, before going to the planning board, return to your evaluation of your lifestyle to help you make your furniture choices. Distressed finishes, for example, are more practical than smoothly finished veneers in a house filled with pets and children. We have mentioned earlier that it is usually more interesting to mix furniture finishes rather than match them. It is also safer, especially for a family that plans to move to larger quarters and to add new pieces to what it already owns. If a present nucleus is a harmonious meld, it will be much easier to add new finishes in future purchases.

It is always a good idea to stay clear of oversized pieces, awkward shapes, or any furniture design that will be difficult to rearrange in a new location.

FURNITURE ARRANGEMENT

A room filled with handsome furniture does not necessarily come together as a cohesive and beautifully integrated interior—not unless the furniture has been properly arranged. By this we mean that all designs should be positioned to provide maximum comfort and living use, and to enable the family to enjoy the room to its full potential. No living room in a private home should ever be comparable to a roped-off model room in a furniture or department store, the kind of display with the unspoken message "Look but don't touch." On the contrary, the careful, skillful, and successful placement of furniture is what makes a room inviting and welcoming—a goal that is critical to every decorating plan.

The harmony, sense of balance, and warmth that greet you when you walk into a truly charming interior should be so natural and ingratiating that one might think that the furniture was placed around in a casual, throwaway manner. Surprisingly, it is just these wonderful "laid-back" interiors that prove to be the result of hours and hours of careful

To allow enough space for a small game/dining table, sofas and chair were positioned on an angle, instead of symmetrically framing the fireplace.

AMERICAN TRADITIONAL

Another catty-corner arrangement, here to make room for a small but comfortable seating nucleus in a master bedroom.

A small dining area is gracefully worked into a corner of a large living space.

Two large chairs are angled toward each other to enhance the comfort and conviviality of this seating group.

AMERICAN TRADITIONAL

planning; the beauty of it is that they don't look that way. Much thought, modification, alteration, reassessment, and trial and error must go into the various stages of working out a meaningful plan. Only such an investment of time and care can pay off in interiors that look relaxed and unstudied.

For a room to work, it must allow for ample traffic patterns and an intelligent use of wall space. By this we mean that a furniture design must not be so huge that it covers every inch of the slice of wall allotted to it, nor should the style in question be tiny or undersized, so that it looks "ditsy" (a professional designer's colloquialism) against a vast wall.

If you are dealing with a living room, a natural focal point such as a fireplace may determine the major furniture groupings. A room with many openings and little wall space will suggest using independent furniture groupings that "float," rather than the perimeter approach (furniture lined up around the wall of a room), which these days, in any case, has pretty much gone out of style.

Solving the space puzzle, in short, takes careful preparation and skillful design; the final blueprint will then be a map you can follow with assurance. As you fill it in at point of purchase, always bear in mind that no matter how perfect it may seem, this blueprint is not set in stone. You can and certainly should make changes as you go along, if you find alternative solutions that seem preferable and will work just as well as some of your original ideas.

We are not talking here about trial and error in the sense of suggesting that you purchase whatever furniture you like and then start moving it around your room until it suddenly comes together in a wonderful arrangement. We mean trial and error, or experimentation, at the early planning stages, when you are working with graph paper, templates, and pencil. We come to that now. With floor plan and elevation, you will know just what designs you need to buy and the approximate dimensions of each and every piece.

HOW TO MAKE A FLOOR PLAN

To make your floor plan, you'll need graph paper (the kind with ¼-inch squares), lead pencil and eraser, colored pencils, a 12-inch ruler, scissors, and a 6-foot folding or metal tape measure. If you want to end up with the room's layout on unlined paper, you'll need tracing paper to place over the graph paper.

1. Your first step is to measure the length of each wall and transfer it in pencil to the graph paper. Have each square represent 1 foot.

2. Next, measure windows, doorways, and closets, and draw them in their exact location on the plan, showing the path of every door's swing.

3. Measure and indicate the location of any significant architectural features (for example, support beams and pipes that jut out in corners and along walls); heating and cooling units; electrical outlets, light switches, and telephones; and special details such as fireplaces and stairs. Your floor plan should now be an exact, two-dimensional reproduction of your room. It should look as if you were positioned high over the room, looking down on it.

4. Note if the room has a focal point. This is the term for its major point of interest, such as a fireplace, a window with a spectacular view, or an especially dramatic window configuration. Not every room possesses a natural focal point, but since any such center of interest functions as a strong visual magnet that ties everything together—especially if the major furniture grouping has been centered around it—if you don't have a natural focal point to work with, it's a good idea to create one. Some possibilities: a large wall hanging or painting over a sofa, a wall unit or decorative hutch filled with a personal collection of treasured plates, a grouping of artwork or a single painting over a handsome and decorative cabinet or console.

5. Now determine the room's natural traffic paths or patterns. These are the most frequently used routes taken through the room by members of the household (and guests) to get from one point to another—from one doorway to another, to closets, to windows, and so on. The strategy of your furniture arrangement should make it easy to move about the room and use it in a comfortable way. Don't overlook the traffic path that goes from the entrance of the room to your focal point. Everyone has a natural tendency to walk toward the focal point, so this lane should be a major consideration in your plan; don't block it with furniture. Allow at least 3 feet of unobstructed space for major paths (through the room, or to its focal point) and 2 feet for minor ones. Mark these routes on your plan with light arrows.

6. Having determined your traffic paths, you will see that they divide the room into separate and distinct areas or zones. The largest zone will be the logical place to position your major conversation nucleus. Smaller zones or areas could then be utilized for a minor seating group, study or desk area, even a small informal dining arrangement.

7. Knowing the zones or parameters within which to place your furniture, you can now bring the dimensions of your furnishings down to the scale of the drawing. So measure the length, depth, and height of the furnishings you are planning to put into the room. Be sure to include any sizable accessories that will stand on the floor, such as large plants or baskets, and floor lamps.

8. Now you'll need to cut out templates to represent every piece of furniture or freestanding accessory you intend to purchase (or use if you already own it). You make these templates from a sheet of colored paper or cardboard, cutting out shapes that correspond to the width and depth of the furniture to be employed. These templates, of course, must be drawn to scale.

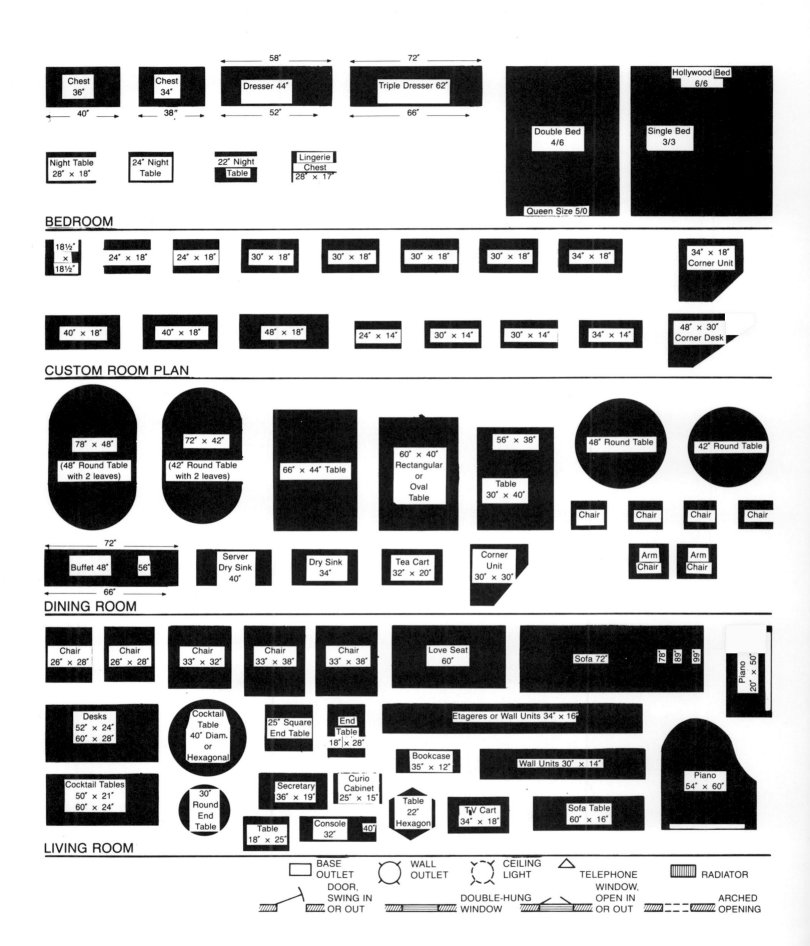

BEDROOM

- Chest 36″ (40″)
- Chest 34″ (38″)
- Dresser 44″ (58″ / 52″)
- Triple Dresser 62″ (72″ / 66″)
- Night Table 28″ × 18″
- 24″ Night Table
- 22″ Night Table
- Lingerie Chest 28″ × 17″
- Double Bed 4/6 / Queen Size 5/0
- Hollywood Bed 6/6 / Single Bed 3/3

CUSTOM ROOM PLAN

- 18½″ × 18½″
- 24″ × 18″
- 24″ × 18″
- 30″ × 18″
- 30″ × 18″
- 30″ × 18″
- 30″ × 18″
- 34″ × 18″
- 34″ × 18″ Corner Unit
- 40″ × 18″
- 40″ × 18″
- 48″ × 18″
- 24″ × 14″
- 30″ × 14″
- 30″ × 14″
- 34″ × 14″
- 48″ × 30″ Corner Desk

DINING ROOM

- 78″ × 48″ (48″ Round Table with 2 leaves)
- 72″ × 42″ (42″ Round Table with 2 leaves)
- 66″ × 44″ Table
- 60″ × 40″ Rectangular or Oval Table
- 56″ × 38″ Table 30″ × 40″
- 48″ Round Table
- 42″ Round Table
- Chair
- Chair
- Chair
- Chair
- Buffet 48″ / 56″ (72″ / 66″)
- Server Dry Sink 40″
- Dry Sink 34″
- Tea Cart 32″ × 20″
- Corner Unit 30″ × 30″
- Arm Chair
- Arm Chair

LIVING ROOM

- Chair 26″ × 28″
- Chair 26″ × 28″
- Chair 33″ × 32″
- Chair 33″ × 38″
- Chair 33″ × 38″
- Love Seat 60″
- Sofa 72″ / 78″ / 89″ / 99″
- Piano 20″ × 50″
- Desks 52″ × 24″ / 60″ × 28″
- Cocktail Table 40″ Diam. or Hexagonal
- 25″ Square End Table
- End Table 18″ × 28″
- Etageres or Wall Units 34″ × 16″
- Cocktail Tables 50″ × 21″ / 60″ × 24″
- 30″ Round End Table
- Secretary 36″ × 19″
- Curio Cabinet 25″ × 15″
- Bookcase 35″ × 12″
- Wall Units 30″ × 14″
- Piano 54″ × 60″
- Table 18″ × 25″
- Console 32″ / 40″
- Table 22″ Hexagon
- TV Cart 34″ × 18″
- Sofa Table 60″ × 16″

BASE OUTLET · WALL OUTLET · CEILING LIGHT · TELEPHONE · RADIATOR
DOOR, SWING IN OR OUT · DOUBLE-HUNG WINDOW · WINDOW, OPEN IN OR OUT · ARCHED OPENING

You may even want to use colored paper at least close to the color in which the furniture will be made, so as to balance the furnishings by color as well as by dimensions; you can thus avoid the mistake of placing all your bright-colored designs on one side of the room and understated neutrals on the other—a mistake that would make the room appear as unbalanced as if you put all the tall furniture designs on one side.

The advantage of working with templates is that they give you the flexibility to arrange and rearrange until you are satisfied with the result. And remember always to take care that cupboard and cabinet doors and drawers can be opened without crowding or discomfort.

ELEVATIONS

After you've done a floor plan, it is also extremely helpful to make elevations of the four walls of your room. An elevation plan will enable you to determine the best balance between high and low pieces placed against the walls.

To make your elevation, first draw the walls, using a separate piece of graph paper to represent each one. Measure the width and height of every wall detail and indicate them in scale on the elevation. Now refer to your floor plan to see which furnishings are placed along the walls. Then make a to-scale (height and length) drawing of each piece in its proper position against the wall.

Now you are ready to examine the furniture placements and judge how good the balance is. Here are some basic guidelines you can follow:

CUT-OUT TEMPLATES

Use these templates and symbols to plan your rooms. Trace and cut out the templates you need (from kraft paper or light cardboard) and fit them into your room plan on graph paper where a ¼-inch square represents 1 foot of floor space.

1. Try to have a variety of elevation on the walls. Avoid the monotony of only one wall level.
2. Keep the walls in balance to each other. In other words, avoid an uneven distribution of furniture.
3. Balance the heights of those furnishings placed against the wall not only with each other but also with the

wall's fixed details (door, windows, built-in bookcases, windows, and the like). Place your furniture to work in tandem with these built-in verticals and horizontals.

4. Keep opposite walls balanced in "strength," if possible. If one oversized armoire is placed on one wall, try to use something equally strong (or a grouping of significant impact) on the opposite wall.

5. Create interesting arrangements on those walls most easily viewed from the major seating areas.

6. Start with the basics, then add to fill whatever space remains to be decorated. Be sure to give furniture groupings the necessary "breathing space." This avoids a sense of crowding and makes them more comfortable and inviting. Upholstered furniture should never actually touch the wall.

7. Look for variety of shapes in table designs. Try for a mix of square, round, rectangular, and oval. It's more interesting.

8. Use furniture arrangement to visually alter the proportions of a long and narrow room (a common high-rise phenomenon). Place a sofa, desk, or cabinet that is finished on all sides perpendicular to a wall in order to divide a room into two areas—say, one for living and the other for dining. Oversized paintings and mirrors, tall screens, French doors, and tall, dramatically dressed windows also contribute to the vertical balance of a room.

Even if you are not planning to redecorate, but want a fresh and new look, you can experiment with templates. Move the templates around on graph paper until you arrive at a satisfactory new arrangement that gives your interior(s) a different look.

When you are mixing furniture finishes, make sure that the mix is executed in a balanced way. Avoid putting all the pale finishes on one side of the room, the furniture in dark or painted finishes on the other. Spread the mix around in an interesting fashion.

Your completed floor plans and elevations may suggest a way of decorating your rooms that is quite different from what you had envisioned—indicating, in all likelihood, that your original idea just wasn't feasible from the standpoints of floor and wall space.

Above all, don't forget about satisfying the needs of your lifestyle. (Again, keep in mind that distressed finishes are more practical for a house filled with pets and children than the more formal smooth and shiny ones.)

Viewing the vast array of truly beautiful fabric textures, patterns, and prints available in today's marketplace can be a visually exciting and memorable experience. Yet shopping in earnest for fabrics

CHAPTER 9

FABRIC PATTERN AND TEXTURE

to complete the decoration of a single room, more so an entire house, can be mind-boggling. How does one sift through these limitless riches to pick those fabrics that will really pull the decorating plan together, that will effectively create the rooms of your dreams?

Our forebears were faced with the opposite problem: choice was nonexistent. The few fabrics available were woven at home, where a hand loom and spinning wheel were conspicuously present. Young girls learned to weave at an early age to help their mothers produce the fabrics needed to clothe the family and cover the furniture.

Weaving is, of course, an ancient art, traceable to those early cultures which first learned how to transform the coats of animals or certain vegetation from the field into thread that could be woven into cloth.

Our American colonists picked up this ancient art and fashioned their own unique and wonderful variations, most of them closely associated with the decorative styles of American interiors just before and after the Revolution. Looms were constructed by the local carpenter, or the head of the household if he was handy enough, and were usually placed in the large kitchen or keeping room.

The dyes for yarns and fabrics referred to in Chapter 3

Overscaled floral print is the single fabric cover of this country living room.

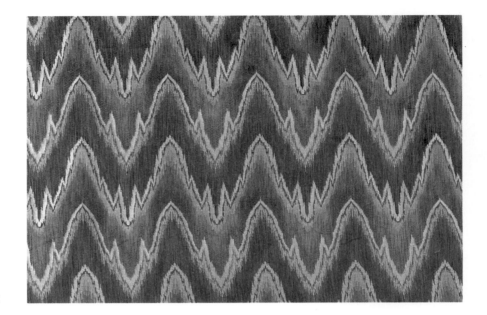

The colors and pattern of the flame stitch, a popular Colonial weave, are emulated in this machine-made contemporary fabric

were the harvest of the colonial housewife, who brewed rich and pleasing hues from assorted plants and trees—dogwood and butternut trees, bittersweet, indigo, goldenrod, blueberries, and other plants. The oranges, reds, blues, greens, and browns squeezed out of these trees, wildflowers, and common garden varieties dominated the coloration of Colonial fabrics.

Jacquard patterns woven on these early looms featured such motifs as geometric designs, eagles, stars, lions, and flowers. These were especially popular for use in making bed coverlets. Later motifs were more intricate—among them, the wonderful patterns of hearts, tulips, and birds.

Sampler work was also an integral part of a young girl's education, for samplers were endemic to the Colonial lifestyle, and all female children were tutored in needlework of every kind. Today, sampler making, except by a few afficionados, seems to be a lost art, but the sampler look still inspires fabric prints that emulate the cross-stitch effect as well as the motifs typical of sampler design.

Most printed cotton fabrics were imported from France until the latter part of the eighteenth century when the technology for printing cloth was developed here. Most of

This jacquard coverlet design is a close copy of those early hand-woven fabrics that were part of every colonist's home.

Stylized flowers and stars, in a striped print design, were inspired by typical motifs of Colonial jacquard weaves.

the topics or themes showcased in these prints were commemorative—a famous battle, a historic event, a great statesman. This industry first emerged in small mill towns in Massachusetts, where birds, floral designs, harvesting themes, foliage, and winter sports were the principal motifs.

A word must also be said here about the art of quilting and the emergence of the American quilt as one of the most popular of today's soft accents in rooms decorated in the American Traditional country style. Even the old-time quilting bees, those coveys of Colonial quilters who got together to work while they socialized, have been revived as a present-day pastime. Cottage industries have also come into existence to meet the ever-growing demand for handmade quilts, now that costs of the antique ones have become so exorbitant. Not only are quilts a dominant facet of our American design heritage, but their unique motifs have had great influence on the design of printed and woven fabrics. Stars, concentric squares, stylized flowers, baskets of flowers, cornucopias, wreaths, pineapples, sunbursts, and schoolhouses were among the special motifs first executed in quilts and then later reinterpreted as fabric design.

Let's return to our original question: how best to ferret out from the overwhelming assortment available those fabrics which will work most successfully in your room. As with all other aspects of interior design, you must exert a discipline, and perhaps most emphatically in the selection of fabrics, where there is so much more to please the eye than you probably have room for.

You must ask yourself certain questions, then let the answers tell you what to select, what to reject. Do you want to use a generous amount of a single fabric pattern, or do you prefer a mix of motifs? Should the major part of the fabrics you choose be textured rather than patterned, or do you want to use equal amounts of each? What kind of look will work best with your furniture, the style and shape of your seating designs, the structure of your window treatments? Is the room to be luxuriously elegant, or should it offer a relaxed and cozy informality? What other patterns are to be added in the form of rugs, paintings, or screens? In making these decisions, try to remember that both pattern and texture are partnered with color. So not only is the design and/or fabric significant, but also the color or colors in which it is expressed. All elements work together to endow a room with its sense of harmony, its individuality, its personality.

PATTERN, THE DYNAMIC INGREDIENT

Pattern is the element or ingredient most responsible for a room's vitality. Expressed in homespun cotton prints or richly elegant brocades, pattern can add immeasurably to the character of an interior. But although as important in its own way as color or texture, pattern should not be automatically chosen for every room in the house. Nor should it be carelessly overlooked. Whether to employ pattern or to avoid its use is a decision that should be carefully considered for each room to be decorated. And remember, too, that even a room which does not contain a specific fabric or wallpaper pattern will usually contain paintings and furniture shapes that provide visual patterns of their own.

Patterned fabric, as we have said, is available today in limitless choice. And it is often used in a seemingly unlimited way—whether covering walls or on lampshades, tables, and cabinets—in addition to its deployment at the windows and on upholstered furniture. Whenever you apply pattern, always consider the three basic factors of color, scale, and line.

The combination of colors in a single pattern is called a colorway. Most manufacturers of printed and woven fabrics offer the same pattern in a choice of colorways, or different patterns in the same range of colorways. These latter groupings, usually referred to as correlated or coordinated collections, make it much easier for you to use more than one pattern in a single room. This approach of using pattern with pattern was favored and applied by professionals almost to excess a few years ago, but when executed with restraint it can produce very appealing interiors. Usually the patterns

ASK YOURSELF . . .

- **Is the room to be elegant or cozy?**

- **Are there other patterns in rugs, furnishings, or screens to be considered?**

- **What is the color scheme of the room?**

CONSIDER . . .

- **using a single fabric pattern**

- **mixing pattern motifs**

- **using textured fabrics**

- **using patterned fabrics with textured fabrics**

within each grouping vary in scale—including, possibly, a small-scale geometric, an oversized floral, and a more moderately scaled floral interpretation.

If you choose a pattern as the starting point of your color scheme, you must, of course, select it before deciding upon the placement of color in other furnishings. Many professionals prefer to use the dominant color of a fabric print or pattern (usually the background tone) for major areas; this works well if the color is muted or neutral, unless a dramatic look is desired. As a rule, the more intense colors are utilized as accents in smaller areas.

As described in our chapter on color, a particular color changes according to the light, the texture in which it is expressed, and the other colors adjacent to it. Nowhere is this more evident than in the way a fabric pattern appears to the eye. Rich, warm tones in a print can be intensified by a strong paint color on the walls or carpeting in a similar hue. The same print can seem much cooler when set among whites and off-whites.

The size and scale of a pattern or repeated motif is another very important consideration. Too much of a large and splashy design will overpower a room and the beautiful furnishings within it, to a point where they cannot even be appreciated. Combining two large-scale patterns can also lead to visual disaster, as the patterns will clash. Small-scale patterns, on the other hand, seem to work well together or in a mix with one large-scale design.

The smaller a pattern, the more likely it is to blend into itself from a distance and appear as a plain texture. Monochromatic interpretations of a pattern also present an allover effect of almost solid color. All patterns tend to "read" differently when used to cover furniture, or as window treatment, bearing little resemblance to the way they looked as flat samples. So be sure to get a large sample of any fabric you are considering and try it out in the room to get some idea of how it will look.

The line direction of a fabric pattern (vertical, horizontal, or diagonal) and the line character (curved, straight, zigzag,

Plaid upholstery texture is used on this adaptation of a high-back Chippendale wing chair.

or undulating) can be helpful decorating tools; they direct the eye. A sofa will seem taller if covered in a vertical stripe, or longer and lower if the pattern is horizontal. Undulating lines are not as animated as zigzags, but both contribute some sense of animation. It makes sense to avoid patterns that are too vibrant or too jarring, although when used minimally they can provide interesting and visually exciting accents.

When choosing a fabric design, take into consideration what other patterns will be selected. The introduction of

The pineapple, a Colonial symbol of hospitality, is the central motif of a contemporary print resembling a stencil design.

fabric motif is usually a plus for any room; it can bring a tired space to life, give cohesiveness to a collection of disparate furniture styles, prevent an interior from being dull and boring. But don't overdo a good thing. Be aware of the size of the room in relation to the kind of pattern you plan to use. For example, a small design used in a large area becomes less significant and has less impact than when chosen for a small room.

If you are using a strongly patterned rug, then choose more subdued motifs in the printed or patterned fabrics elsewhere in the room.

Pattern, in much the same way as color, changes its effect when applied in quantity. Surprisingly, a somewhat strong design will seem less boisterous when applied generously; used this way, it seems to tone itself down. When less of it is utilized, on the other hand, it may pop out dramatically.

If you want one pattern to dominate in a room of mixed patterns, choose the major design first, then coordinate the other patterns around it. Good secondary patterns include checks, stripes, small-scale geometrics, and country designs.

For rooms adjacent to each other, it may be wise to relate

One of today's versions of the paisley pattern, an American Traditional favorite, is expressed here in a colorful print used to cover a large wing chair.

them in your use of pattern, in much the same way that you would handle their color schemes, in order to avoid a jarring effect.

Don't throw all your patterned fabrics over to one side of the room—for example, by placing a print-covered sofa before a wide window draped in the same print. Use chairs, pillows, or table skirts to pull pattern over to the other side of an interior for balance.

TEXTURE, THE SUBTLE INGREDIENT

Texture, although just as important as pattern, is less dramatic in its immediate impact. Texture refers primarily to

BEFORE YOU BEGIN . . .

Take paint chips and small swatches of wallpaper, rugs, and fabrics and glue them together on a single piece of paper. This will enable you to judge whether the colors will blend harmoniously or compete in the room.

KEEP IN MIND . . .

- In a room of very little pattern, it is important to employ a diversity of textures.

- In a subdued color scheme, textural variety can be enormously effective, even necessary.

- The allover use of pattern on walls, windows, and furniture can make a room seem larger.

- More intense colors are better used as accents in smaller areas.

the tactile sense of touch, but we experience texture through our eyes as well as through our fingers. Textures establish or enhance the mood of a room. Velvets, silks, and satins immediately convey an elegant formality, while rough-woven fabrics transmit a casual and rustic message.

All fabrics, even those printed with motifs or woven with patterns, have texture. Some textures, such as tweeds, wools, linens, and homespuns, are rougher in feeling, while polished cottons, silks, and silklike synthetics lend a smoother touch.

Some fabrics are flat; others, such as velvet, have a pile weave.

Using texture effectively adds additional dimension to a room. In a room that has no or very little pattern, it is crucial to employ a diversity of texture. A play on texture will provide an interior with visual interest, will keep it from appearing dull. Too many textures, on the other hand, can produce an uneasy, nervous effect.

Before you make a final commitment to your fabrics, get a good idea of how their textures will work with other textures in the room. Professional designers take small swatches of the wallpaper, rugs, fabrics, and paint chips for a room and glue them together on a single piece of paper so that they can see all the colors, textures, and patterns together and thereby judge whether they blend or fight. Such a sheet can also be useful in helping you to remember all the elements with which you are working. In making the final selections, however, don't overlook the color and texture of your furniture as well.

The introduction of pattern and texture, whether to a large or a limited degree, will play a significant role in the final look of your room. Both elements add a sense of movement and dimension that can be lacking if all surfaces are of solid color (no patterns) or are made of the same material (no textural contrast). They can and should be used to compensate or play off against other elements of the decorating plan. In a subdued color scheme, for example, textural variety can be enormously effective and necessary. An exquisitely drawn fabric print, applied abundantly, can draw the eye away from pedestrian, run-of-the-mill furnishings. The allover use of pattern, when put on walls, at windows, and on all the furniture, can make a room seem considerably larger.

Unless it affords sufficient storage, the beauty of a home can fall apart. An overflow of possessions will produce chaos and clutter from one room to another. Only when there is a place for everything,

CHAPTER 10
STORAGE AND DUAL-PURPOSE FURNITURE

and everything is in its place, does a home offer the comfort and harmony so conducive to enjoyable and workable day-to-day living.

Architects and builders are fully aware of how important a priority adequate storage is to the average contemporary family, which today possesses a greater diversity of assorted paraphernalia and belongings to be stored on shelves, or out of sight, than ever before. Storage must be organized, must hold and display clothing, linens, china, crystal, and silver, as well as a wide spectrum of electronics, sports gear, and hobby equipment; the list goes on and on.

The early colonists had such meager belongings that all they needed was humble cupboards, wooden chests, presses, and wardrobes—the first storage styles to emerge in seventeenth-century America. Eventually, of course, cabinetry became a highly refined art, and designs grew more copious and versatile. The most outstanding examples of eighteenth-century Queen Anne and Chippendale artistry were storage styles such as the broken-pediment highboy and the block-front chest, as well as exquisite secretaries and desks. The

Bookshelf cabinets in a dark pine finish provide drawer space for storage of clothing in a vacation-house bedroom.

high sideboards of Sheraton and Hepplewhite that came later were favored for the more formal dining rooms of affluent urban Americans. Paneled walls often included recesses or niches specifically designed to hold books or porcelains.

The type of storage available to us today falls roughly into three categories: freestanding cabinets, modular storage, and built-in storage. To determine what kinds of storage you need, and how much of each kind will suffice, you must first assess the quantity and variety of your possessions and ascertain how much of your storage requirements can be satisfied by the closets of your house and any furniture you already own. Then set up a simple mathematical equation: what you have subtracted from what you need equals what you must buy or build.

You will know, of course, whether you intend to stay in your present apartment or house for many years, or if it is only a way station. This will guide your planning and accounting for any built-in furniture that becomes part of the house, or any that cannot travel with you should you move.

Pre–World War II apartments and houses were usually built with a substantial amount of closet space, but with the rising costs of construction materials and labor in the decades that followed, many builders economized on the storage space allocated for new living areas. This "closet economy" has obviously exacerbated the problem of dealing with one's more extensive and diverse possessions.

Once you have established a floor plan for your rooms—either as a "from scratch" blueprint or as a scheme that mixes the designs you presently own with those you intend to buy—you must evaluate it in terms of total storage potential. Before making a single purchase, determine whether or not you really have enough such space. A word of advice: most people tend to underestimate how much storage they really need.

If you do not have enough, you will have to make "strategic substitutions"—that is, you will have to replace one or more pieces of furniture that have been scheduled for purchase with some other, more storage-worthy designs. Some examples: a highboy instead of a low chest; compact cabinets or even a desk to replace one or both nightstands; a storage headboard rather than a simple bedstand; a small chest substituting for an end table next to a sofa.

You may also be able to discover new places to add storage designs without having to alter your original floor plan. A chest might be fitted in at the end of a bed, a decorative trunk positioned under a coffee table or console design. While you are doing this, reevaluate your seating vis-à-vis storage. Are you allowing too much of one and too little of the other? Can some modification rectify the imbalance? If so, do it now, before you have bought anything.

FREESTANDING STORAGE FURNITURE

Today's repertoire of freestanding cabinet designs such as chests, highboys, and secretaries are among the most outstanding interpretations of American Traditional styling at its finest. The earlier designs contained only drawers and were simple chests to hold personal belongings in the humble living rooms, dining rooms, and bedrooms of those first colonists. Later cabinetry was designed with both drawers and doors in order to contain a wider diversity of possessions.

Manufacturers of American Traditional furniture in the 1980s, cognizant of contemporary needs, are outfitting many of their cabinets with compartments to hold audio and video equipment, or to serve as a bar or fully equipped entertainment center. Many designs contain pull-out swivel shelves to present a television set for easy viewing.

New adaptations of hutches and china cabinets continue a tradition of beautiful dining storage popular for hundreds of years. Today's interpretations, especially the china cabinets, are marvelously engineered and compartmentalized, often with adjustable shelves, glass doors, and interior lighting.

Multiples of grill-door library units are bunched together to form a long storage wall in an apartment dining room.

Buffet or serving cabinets, which first emerged during the proliferation of the Sheraton style, are today lower and, if desired, longer. If space permits, they can be a welcome addition to the dining room, or to a living room utilized for buffet entertaining.

The imposing highboy is still a perennial favorite, first because it offers so much storage potential, and secondly because it adds true American Traditional flavor to any room in which it appears. Another traditional favorite that makes efficient use of space is the decorative corner cabinet, which has the added reward of a built-in look.

For needed bedroom storage, manufacturers offer the copious double and triple dressers that combine drawer and cabinet space. While such cabinets did not exist in Colonial days, they represent the continuing attempt by realistic furniture producers to satisfy contemporary living requirements within the framework of American Traditional design.

One of the best ways to augment the storage potential of your home, and at the same time add more interest to your rooms, is to be flexible and avoid labeling furniture as useful only for a specific room—dining room, living room, or bedroom. Almost all freestanding furniture designs can go anywhere in the house. An armoire will offer abundant storage for your bedroom, but it can also perform splendidly as a china-and-crystal cabinet in the dining room, or an entertainment center in the family room. By the same token, chests or any furniture that contains only drawers can move out of the bedroom and into the hall, foyer, hobby area, breakfast room, or bathroom.

Dry sinks and hutches, cherished Colonial favorites, can also play other than their traditional roles. Dry sinks are delightful hall or family-room accents, and new versions of the hutch, available in a superb range of wood and painted finishes, can store clothing, books, and other personal collectibles in a bedroom, or be deployed for both open and concealed storage in a living room or family area.

MODULAR FURNITURE

The term "modular storage furniture" refers to a variety of individual modules or units massed together to compose a wall system that can be either extensive or modest, depending upon how many modules are used.

A contemporary concept, such modular systems are expressed in a diversity of American Traditional styles, and in a wide choice of wood and painted finishes. For those who prefer the flexibility of freestanding furniture and the look of a built-in, modular systems are superb strategies for solving the space crunch. These marvelous designs climb walls,

MODULAR WALL STORAGE

- Built-in effect at half the cost of customized furnishings
- Creates architectural interest
- Ideal for hobby corners
- Can be used in place of chest and dresser in the bedroom
- Can be easily moved

LIBRARY AND BOOKSTACK UNITS

- May be moved from room to room or place to place
- Can carry a wall arrangement around a corner within one room or into another

BUILT-IN FURNITURE

- More space-efficient than any other kind of storage design
- Maximizes storage potential of existing wall area
- Provides vertical accent
- Can camouflage ugly defects and protrusions such as pipes, radiators, air conditioners, jogs, beams, blemished walls
- Can blend in when painted either the major wall color or accent tone

snuggle under windows, turn corners, or frame a window, all without eating up precious floor space. Beautifully engineered upper and lower elements fit together with the flexibility of building blocks, and can be rearranged and reassembled when moved to a new home. Since manufacturers keep most collections in their line for years, you can start with a few modules and add when space and money permit.

With modular wall storage you not only get a built-in effect at half the custom cost, you create instant architectural enrichment and solve any of a dozen different storage requirements.

Modular units are designed with drawers and cabinets in the lower, or base, modules, while upper units contain open shelves as well as closed cabinet area. The upper units are shallower than the lower ones upon which they rest. This allows the top of the base cabinet to proffer additional and deeper open display/storage space.

Manufacturers produce these traditionally styled modules with interiors engineered to hold television or stereophonic equipment, serve as a bar, incorporate a desk or a console table that can pull out from the wall, conceal a complete work center with file drawers and typewriter table, or open into a beautifully compartmented sewing "room" behind louvered cabinet doors.

These wall systems are offered with occasional-table designs in the same styling and finishes, so you can put together a whole room of matching wood pieces—an arrangement sometimes effective for achieving a feeling of greater space.

Not only do modular wall systems create full-fledged hobby corners and activity areas: they can also be used in the bedroom in place of the obligatory chest and dresser when abundant storage is required. Modular walls are often the answer to a storage crisis in a studio or small one-bedroom apartment. Here they can be placed in the living room, then reassigned to a family room or child's room when there is a move to larger quarters.

Modular storage designs contain upper and lower cabinets, a desk, and a special sewing unit that transforms an upstairs sitting room into a useful hobby center.

LIBRARY, OR BOOKSTACK, UNITS

Library, or "bookstack," units can be used singly, in pairs, or in as many multiples as are necessary to compose an entire wall. They are less flexible than modular wall systems, since each library unit is a single vertical element, rather than an arrangement of upper and lower modules.

Manufacturers of American Traditional furniture have expressed these copious storage units in handsome adaptations of period styling, ranging from the most formal Chippendale and Queen Anne designs in cherry and other fruitwood finishes to country-mood oak, pine, and maple interpretations.

Some library units are composed exclusively of book-

Stackables can be arranged as you like. Here they store books and stereo components on open shelves and assorted belongings in drawers and behind cabinet doors.

shelves; others feature framed glass doors on the upper part of the cabinet, above solid doors to conceal whatever storage is placed below. Many units combine open shelving on top with doors or drawers in the lower cabinet area.

Such designs are as exquisitely detailed as any other finely crafted freestanding furniture style. Paneled doors, dentil molding, and authentically wrought pulls and hinges distinguish many of these imposing designs. They give a room the architectural effect of built-ins, plus an enormous amount of storage potential. In addition, library collections often contain units that have been specially engineered to make the wall arrangement turn a corner.

Best of all, when you move, you can take it all with you.

BUILT-IN FURNITURE

The beauty of built-ins is that they are more space-efficient than any other kind of storage design. They maximize the storage potential of existing wall areas, creating fabulous storage walls or otherwise putting dead space to work in surprising ways.

The heritage of built-in furniture in America began with the Shakers, a functional and utility-minded people who devised some of our earliest examples of truly efficient kitchen tools and household equipment. In the Shaker communes that exist today only as museums, we see many examples of extensive built-in wall cupboards, simple in design, which may run from floor to ceiling and may sometimes cover an entire wall.

There are many storage units that can be built as home-handyman projects, using modestly priced lumber and a couple of cans of paint. But no project of this nature should be attempted unless one has the necessary know-how, or is handy and able to apply the necessary instructions from books or magazines.

A custom job, however, does not have to be an elegant affair, produced from exquisite woods and up to the design and finish of finest furniture. A professional carpenter can use low-cost plywood, which can then be painted to blend in or contrast with the wall color of the room.

A custom storage design can provide closets where none existed; it can merely frame a window, or produce a super wall of storage space that includes shelf, cabinet, and closet areas.

In place of one large china cabinet, a storage wall of upper and lower cabinets (with recessed lighting set in under the upper shelves) can present an unbroken line of serving surface, as well as offer an impressive amount of storage for all dining-room accoutrements.

Building in storage not only multiplies the space potential of any room: it can also provide vertical accent and rich character. A wall of bookshelves enhances a nondescript bedroom that has been converted into a home office; a pair of floor-to-ceiling closet cabinets or armoires creates a niche for a sofa or a bed.

Custom built-ins can be designed so that they camouflage ugly defects and protrusions such as pipes, air conditioners, old-fashioned radiators, jogs, beams, badly blemished walls, even a useless undersized window.

Unless made of attractively grained wood that can be given a stained finish, built-in units should be painted—usually in the major wall color, or in an accent tone. Depending upon the extent of built-in storage you require, it may be more economical and effective in the long run to hire a professional rather than do it yourself. Get some estimates, and contrast these costs with what it would cost you in both materials *and time.*

The installation of side brackets set into verticals can make the shelves of any built-in unit completely adjustable; this feature is often offered in modular bookshelf units.

In selecting freestanding furniture or designing built-ins, you should decide in advance how much open storage (shelf space) you want, and how much concealed storage area is desirable. Your needs will depend upon the nature of your possessions, the location of your home (whether in the dust-free country or grit-ridden city), and your willingness to dust open shelves and whatever is placed upon them on a regular basis.

DUAL-PURPOSE FURNITURE

The hidden guest room, a fact of life in more and more American homes, has been made viable largely by the development of the dual-purpose sleep sofa or convertible. Cleverly engineered to look like garden-variety sofas, and offered in just as many style choices, these convertibles make it pos-

Compact storage is offered by modular units in a white finish for a small area that can be used for living, dining, study, games, or paperwork.

sible to live comfortably in a one-room apartment, to create an additional bedroom in the family or living room, or to put up unexpected guests in the living room without notice.

Sleep sofas can be part of any conventional furniture grouping; since manufacturers usually offer the same design both as a convertible and as a regular sofa without the sleep mechanism, a pair of sofas, one a convertible, can flank a fireplace or picture window. Regular daybeds also offer dual-purpose use, but convert only to a single bed so are not as versatile as the sleep sofas.

Other popular dual-purpose furniture designs include upholstered chairs that rock, swivel, and recline. These are offered in American Traditional styling with a newer and trimmer look that belies the chair's multiple functions.

Whenever you purchase dual-purpose furniture, be sure to look for durability, good construction, and comfort; bargains are usually short-lived. You can expect to pay more for a sleep sofa or swivel chair than you would for their single-purpose counterparts—understandably, given the extra mechanisms.

An old favorite that has returned to the scene as a result of today's space shortage is the wall bed, or Murphy bed, now offered in handsome wall cabinets and in a variety of styles and finishes.

One of the most endearing Colonial designs to survive today is the chair-table: a chair with a round wood back that flops down to become a tabletop.

The gateleg table, a contribution of the William & Mary period, and drop-leaf designs, a Queen Anne innovation, are both doing splendidly today, helping to make use of limited space in a maximum way.

Conversely, many modern table concepts have been expressed in American Traditional styling. These include expandable and flip-top dining tables, bunching and nesting occasional tables, sofa tables (placed behind a sofa), and the ever-popular tea cart.

PART THREE
DECOR-ATING THE ROOMS OF YOUR HOME

You have now reached that point in your decorating project where you are at last ready to put your newly gained expertise to work for you. You have become articulate about the significant style periods that comprise our American Traditional design heritage. You have also absorbed the basic guidelines—the do's and don'ts of how to start your decorating project—and have become familiar with the talents of color, the fundamentals of background design and material. You have learned how to design floor plans and elevations from which to work out the most appropriate furniture choices and arrangements. What is most important, you have come to terms with the comfort, style, and storage needs of your family, and are able to interpret these requirements in the way you decorate your home.

There is no single formula, however, that you can develop and apply to every one of your rooms. Each room has its own specific architecture and size, and each area is used for a special purpose: living, dining, sleeping, home study, and so on. Each kind of room presents its own set of problems; poses its own, often puzzling, decorating challenges. These challenges must be dealt with separately and individually, within the framework of the home in its entirety, so that there is a consistency of style, mood, and, to a certain extent, color.

Your home will be decorated with American Traditional furnishings. But to what degree? If the approach is purist, then you would be expressing this mood in the majority of your rooms (with the possible exception of a family room). If you prefer a more mixed effect, possibly with some contemporary designs worked in, then there can be more diversity of mood from room to room, since your approach will be looser, and will encourage a certain amount of flexibility. Avoid, however, too sudden a change of mood. A living room decorated in a relaxed blend of traditional and contemporary designs should not spill open to a dining room that is a carbon copy of an elegantly formal Queen Anne setting.

For some rooms, you will be starting off with a number of designs already in your possession, carried over from a previous house or apartment. For other areas, you will be working from scratch. Whatever the case, it usually pays to go slowly and not try to buy everything in a rush.

Large and spacious bedrooms and dining rooms suggest that they be used for more than one purpose, and part of the challenge will be to decide how to deal with this extra space in order to make these rooms more useful and efficient. Shortage of space within the home may also encourage you to turn one room or more into dual-purpose areas—living rooms into hidden guest rooms, foyers to double for elegant dining.

The guiding discipline for all your choices will be your family's lifestyle and personal requirements. Along with these are the considerations of comfort, ease of maintenance, and durability, all expressed in a decorative style that pleases the eye and delights the spirit of your family and those friends and guests who come to call.

The living room is the center of the house; its style and spirit express all the facets of a family's special personality and way of life. Because it is almost always the largest single space in any

CHAPTER 11
LIVING ROOMS

home and the most important, it usually costs more to decorate than any other room.

The nature of a living room's decoration, fortunately, lends itself to much wider interpretation than other rooms of the home. A bedroom must contain a bed and the requisite number of storage pieces. A dining room is furnished with a large table, as many chairs as can comfortably be placed around it, and whatever storage furniture can be accommodated. But a living room serves first and foremost as a place for the family to spend time together, or to enjoy a chat with friends. It is also the room where parties are held in conjunction with the dining room—tea parties, dinner parties, cocktail parties, supper parties—whether you entertain on a grand or a limited scale.

Obviously, every living room must have seating furniture and sufficient table surface to hold lamps, glasses, and accessories. If space permits, a desk, cabinet, or server should also be included for its special qualities of function and storage, as well as for necessary balance. But this balance, to a certain extent, is optional. One family might want to put the emphasis almost entirely upon seating furniture, to the exclusion of all but a few tables, whereas another might use its living room to showcase a beautifully designed cabinet or a handsome writing table and chair, and keep its seating designs to a minimum. It may do this because its entertaining

Warm and inviting country living room includes such favorites as a Welsh cupboard, a Windsor rocker, and ladderback chairs. Drop-leaf table behind sofa opens for dining.

commodes will generate a more animated and less predictable composition. Combine these same tables with a camelback or Sheraton sofa and the result would be far more reserved and disciplined.

Tables can also make a difference, and while a certain proportion of these should be in American Traditional styling in order to preserve the predominant mood of the room, you might want to introduce a glass-topped table with a chrome or brass base, or possibly a console design in a bold lacquer.

Such "variations on a theme" would be the way you could exercise your own special talents or decorating flair, as well as the way to give much-cherished designs the vitality and sparkle of today's lifestyles.

Also be sure, wherever it's possible, to vary the shapes of furniture. If the sofa is hard-edged and streamlined, soften it with a round or oval coffee table. If you are searching for a less conventional look, use a grouping of three small tables instead of a single large one.

If your seating group contains a sofa bed, always be sure to choose a coffee table that is not too heavy, so that it can be easily moved away when the bed has to be pulled out from the sofa.

In working out the floor plan and elevations for the living room, you established the structure within which to choose and place your furniture. Existing openings such as windows and doors will set certain limits on the size of tables, cabinets, or upholstered designs to be placed against the walls. Traffic lanes, and the need to create ample air or breathing space around the major conversation groupings, will also define where furniture can and cannot be positioned. But above and beyond these limitations, you can express your own personal taste and room-arrangement strategy.

Seating groups are usually built around a natural focal point, or one which you have to create that will serve the same purpose. The most common natural focal point, of course, is a fireplace, preferably a wood-burning one. Because

A mix of furniture designs, lively hothouse colors, and a heavily textured area rug give this traditional living room its eclectic style.

Furniture in this California living room is positioned to gain a view of the garden and the bay beyond. Except for the love seat, all seating pieces are covered in the same lively floral print.

furniture arrangements are so warm and inviting when centered around a hearth, this architectural element is a key selling point when a house or cooperative apartment is being shown to prospective buyers.

Without a fireplace, as is the case in many of today's new houses and high-rise apartments, you can create your own focal point to serve the same purpose. A magnificent oversized armoire, a painting hung over a blockfront chest, one marvelous window treatment that frames a view of a spectacular garden are all possible focal points. So is a painted Colonial hutch filled with a superb collection of redware or majolica. Even a beautiful sofa, placed before an exquisitely detailed and multipaneled screen, or in front of a window recess filled with trees and plants, can serve as an anchor for a memorable furniture grouping.

Seating arrangements that float do not need a fireplace or any other kind of focal point. Such groupings are held down by area rugs or carpets, and are self-contained and independent of the wall architecture, although they must permit adequate traffic lanes to be channeled around them, and should be positioned so that they are comfortable and inviting. The ways you arrange these islands will also define the way people will group together in your living room, how and where they will face each other or sit next to each other.

Upholstered furniture can also divide the space of a living room into two separate and distinct areas. A sofa set at a right angle to a wall marks off the end of the living area and the start of the dining space. Cabinetry that is finished on all sides, such as a writing table, desk, or étagère, can also accomplish this purpose.

In addition to the major seating group or groups in a living room, there will be smaller or subsidiary arrangements. There might be a single chair or a pair of matched or unmatched chairs and a table. Such subsidiary groupings can be pulled into the major conversation arrangements, especially when there are not enough people in the room to divide into two separate groups.

A bright medley of prints and patterns creates a living-room arrangement built around an upholstered window seat.

While you probably love American Traditional decorating (or you would not be reading this book), you may not love every American Traditional room you have ever seen or clipped out from a magazine. Before finalizing your living-room plan, go back to those clippings of favorite rooms and look more closely at their window treatments, color schemes, furniture designs and groupings, and carpets and area rugs. There may be something very special about the way these rooms were decorated that made you cut them

One large living space incorporates the major seating arrangements for dining area and kitchen. Furniture placement marks the limits of each area.

SUMMARIES AND POINTERS

- As the center of any home or apartment, a living room must have not only seating areas and table surfaces, but charm as well. It is the one room in the house into which you most often welcome friends. It is less important to abide strictly by one motif, finish, or style than to mix and blend to create an interesting room. This includes varying the shapes of furniture as well.

- To divide a grand space so that it's adequate to serve as both a living room and a dining room, you can use either upholstered furniture, such as a sofa placed perpendicular to a wall, or cabinetry finished on all sides. With area rugs and intimate seating groups you can create a conversational area inside this large room.

- Use colors and patterns as your taste dictates in your living room, but be careful to balance the distribution. Try to avoid putting all the color and pattern on one side of the room.

- To expand the potential of your living room, consider freeing the wall

out in the first place. A fresh look at these photographs will probably spark your memory, so that you rediscover certain decorating ideas which you found instantly appealing and can now incorporate into your decorating plan. Such ideas could simply be the placement of a tall table behind a sofa, or an original way to juxtapose accessories on a coffee table, or perhaps some ways to use large baskets for extra storage, or hang a framed quilt instead of a painting over a low cabinet.

In decorating your living room, as we have suggested in our chapters on furniture and fabric choice, you will be using as much or as little pattern as your preferences dictate. Color and pattern should be applied in a balanced effect; you do not want all the bright or strong colors on one side of the room, and neither should you place pattern in a lopsided manner—with too much of a fabric print used at the window as well as on furniture centered around the window.

As you develop your furniture arrangement, you may find it necessary to alter your original fabric scheme. If you decide to use a grouping of seating modules instead of two sofas, you might prefer to change the fabric cover to something plain or textured plain, instead of the print you first chose for the sofas. If, for some reason, you switch over from Oriental or patterned area rugs to plain wall-to-wall carpeting, you would need to introduce more pattern into your fabrics.

One of the advantages of placing furniture out in the room is that it frees wall space for other uses. A tall but narrow highboy or secretary requires only a limited slice of a wall, yet can add needed storage space and much character to a traditional living room.

If space is relatively limited and you have chosen two or three different kinds of seating designs (such as a sofa, two chairs, and an ottoman) to complete the arrangement, you can cover them all in the same decorative print in order to unify these different styles and create a feeling of spaciousness.

space by grouping sectional sofas, chairs, and ottomans in the center of the room. Try to add expandable furniture—such as a drop-leaf coffee table which can be small enough for cocktails for two or large enough to accommodate hors d'oeuvre for four when needed.

Ottomans and benches are wonderful additions to seating groups because they expand the seating potential of an interior, are not imposing, and being backless, can be sat upon to face in any direction. An ottoman added to a wing chair gives a living room additional warmth and cozy hearthside charm. A long low bench can be placed across from a love seat and a matching twin positioned at a right angle to it. When they are joined by two pull-up chairs and a skirted table, the grouping offers ample seating space in an interior of limited size.

To enhance the enjoyment of your room, try to add expandable furniture wherever possible—a drop-leaf coffee table, a gateleg occasional table, a sofa table if space permits, a small chest against a narrow but unused bit of wall.

Make sure that you achieve variety in your choice of chairs. Don't make them all wing or completely upholstered designs; have a balanced mix of upholstered and occasional designs. These occasional chairs are so light that guests can easily move them around if they want to join in on a conversation and there is no more room on the sofa.

And talking about chairs, let us remind you to put as much time and effort into the choice of these designs as you do into the tables and sofas you select. Chairs are for everyone. We seek the haven and comfort of a favorite chair at the end of a busy day. We tell a child his first bedtime stories as we nestle down with him in our most comfortable chair. And we direct our guests to our chairs as well as sofas when we suggest that they make themselves at home.

In early Colonial houses, dining usually took place in the keeping room, a large kitchen or cooking area with a huge hearth, beehive baking oven, and brick or wood floor. There was always a

CHAPTER 12
DINING ROOMS

well-stoked fire going, where dinner was cooked in large cast-iron pots and kettles hung on trammels from a pole or crane. Herbs were dried on racks suspended above the mantel, or hung from the ceiling beams.

As the colonists prospered, they added a full dining room, and the keeping room/kitchen became a dining area for the family's servants.

While many of us today have separate dining rooms, we also seem to have come full circle to the keeping rooms of old. Space-efficient houses are often built with combination kitchen-dining areas. For the colonists, this economy was critical; for us, given the cost of building these days, it has become a new architectural trend. Abetting this trend there is also the increasing prevalence of the working wife/mother, who prefers to prepare her meals within sight and sound of family and guests, instead of being hidden away in a separate and often distant kitchen.

Today's American Traditional dining room may be a full dining room, a dining room/kitchen, or if space is really at a premium, a dining alcove or dining foyer. Whatever, we have learned to adjust our decorating techniques for dining to the size, shape, and various practical propensities of the area in which it is to take place. The fact that a dining space is neither large nor separate does not mean it cannot

An unconventional approach to dining-room decoration: skirted tables made from plywood rounds and covered with a delicate floral print.

be as handsome and sparkling as a full dining room.

The American Traditional dining rooms that we decorate for our own homes can be close approximations of the handsome interiors in which our ancestors entertained their guests. Or we can follow the more conventional format of placing the table in the center of the room and adding a china cabinet and server, but introduce, at the same time, some contemporary elements in the form of the color mix, the wall covering, the fabrics, the carpet or rug. We can go even further from the so-called authentic approach by actually arranging our dining rooms in a totally novel way, and by choosing modern design concepts specially created in American Traditional styling.

One thing is certain: today's American dining room should be both festive and memorable. If the living room is the center of family comfort and conviviality, then the dining room is the heart of family dining and entertaining. This is the last place in the house where you should use a subdued or bland approach; the total look should be both welcoming and scintillating, for dining is a gregarious event, one that celebrates either the family's coming together at the end of the day or the arrival of special friends and other guests. It is an event no matter what the occasion—a Thanksgiving dinner for twenty, or the evening meal for a family of four.

Dining should also be flexible; you should be able to harness your dining space for a formal dinner party, for a buffet supper, or simply to feed a few guests or unexpected extras. There should be ample serving area for platters—especially if you're inclined to buffet dining, which has become such a popular mode of entertaining, with servants now so costly and hard to come by.

Dining-room design must also be an expression of your family's tastes and entertaining patterns. If your favorite fashion is blue jeans and you love to give casual dinners after Sunday football games, you'll hardly want a formal Sheraton- or Adam-style dining room, no matter how much that look appeals to you. You should go with your predominant living preferences when you decide upon the look for your dining room or area.

Ask yourself the same kinds of questions discussed in our chapter on lifestyles, only now be a bit more specific. Do you like formal or informal dinners? How much storage do you need for linens, flatware, china, and the like? How often do you entertain? Are most of your parties limited to six or eight all told, or do you prefer big cocktails-through-dinner events, handled buffet fashion? How often is your dining room used during the day, and on weekends? Do you have small children, and therefore need durable, stainproof fabrics and easy-care flooring? What is the style and color scheme of the adjacent living room to which it must relate? What are its architectural assets and defects?

The answers to all these questions, plus your own taste preferences, should point the way toward the design direction that will work best for you and your family. Obviously, what you choose in terms of actual furniture will be limited by the architectural layout of the room or area. The larger the space, the more ample the wall area, and the more opportunity you will have to choose and position such storage designs as china cabinets or hutches and serving cabinets. If wall space is limited, you may not be able to position more than one such cabinet.

As with the arrangement of living-room furniture, you will also be striving for a balanced and aesthetically pleasing look for your dining room. Avoid putting an overload of cabinets on one wall, even if there is enough space for them. Do not select your cabinets before you have decided where to place the dining-room table. After all, you may not want to put it where it usually goes—in the center of the room. If your room has a magnificent view, you might wish to place the table closer to the window. Or perhaps you are planning to create a small sitting area on one side of a large dining room—this would automatically position the table off-center, and therefore affect what other furniture could be placed with the room.

Professionals often use a more imaginative design ap-

THREE TYPES OF DINING-ROOM ARRANGEMENTS:

1. Apartment layout with living room and kitchen
2. Dining room that doubles as a work space
3. Dining alcove off traditional living room

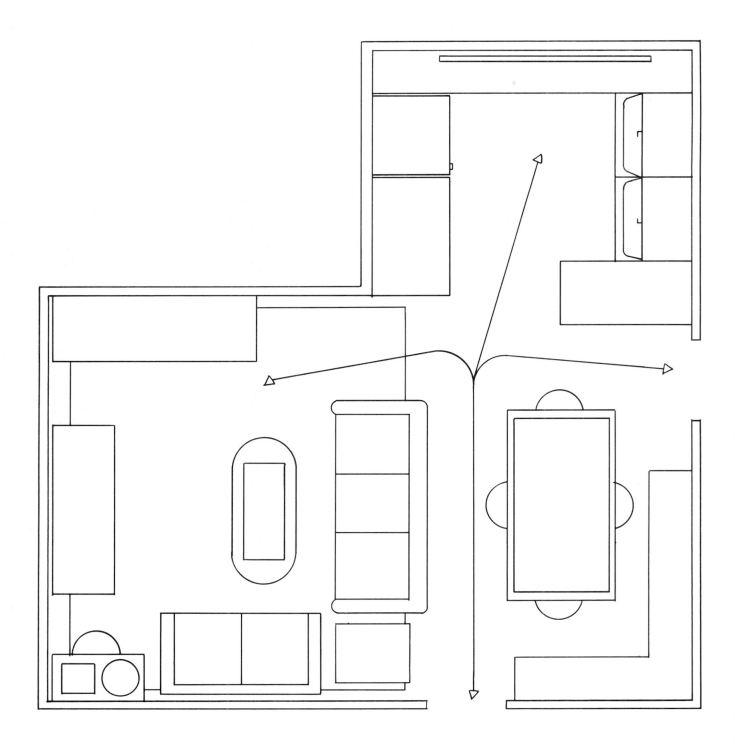

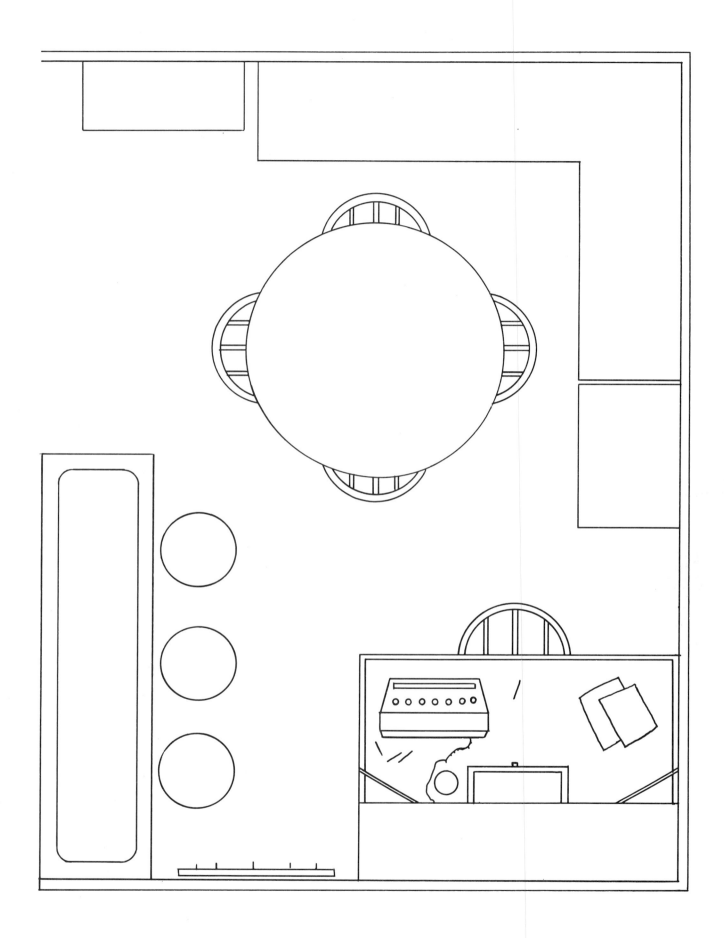

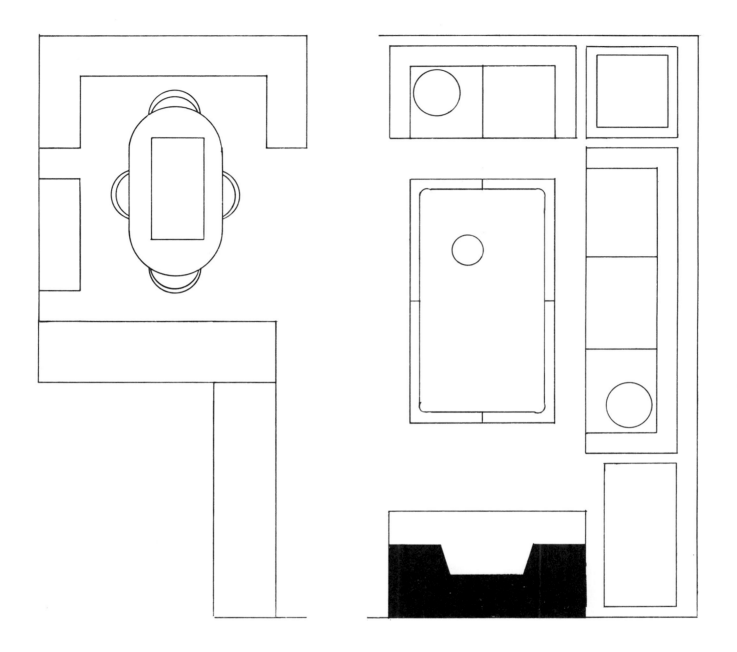

proach for the dining room than for any other room of the house, even when working with American Traditional furniture. They will select two round tables rather than one long and expandable rectangular one. This is done usually for two reasons: visually, such an arrangement will make a long and narrow room seem better proportioned; and quite often a family has found that small groups work better, conversationally, than one large gathering.

In choosing the furniture for your dining room, also consider the choice that is available in sizes and shapes, as well as in design and finish. Dining tables are offered in a variety of sizes; many new American Traditional tables are deliberately scaled to suit the small dining areas that are typically found in new apartments and condominiums.

Dining tables can be shaped square, oblong, hexagonal, round, or oval. The dimensions of your dining room or area, and the amount of hard-edged furniture that is to be included in the room, should guide you in the choice of your table shape.

The quiet refinement of Colonial dining is reinterpreted in furniture adapted from classic period designs. Center to this dining room is gateleg-table reproduction.

Conventionally, American Traditional dining rooms have been decorated, more or less, by a pat formula. A table surrounded by the requisite number of chairs is placed in the center of the room under a chandelier. If wall space allows, both a china cabinet and a server or low buffet are also included. All pieces are in the same style and finish, chosen from the same matched furniture group or collection by a single manufacturer.

This type of decorating, while safe and sure, can also be quite pedestrian. If you follow this route—unless you use great imagination and innovation in your choice of floor treatment, window design, wall coverings, and fabric selection—your dining room will be almost a clone of other dining rooms decorated in this same but uninspiring manner.

Many homeowners decorate their dining rooms in this "matched suite" approach simply because it is how they have seen the furniture displayed on the floor where it is sold. Retailers showcase their furniture this way to make it easier for their customers to see everything available within a specific dining-room collection. But a perusal of current decorating magazines and books will demonstrate that the prettiest, most interesting, and most personal American dining rooms are not treated with this matched effect. A hutch may be in a painted finish, the dining table may be a dark oak, the chairs in stripped pine.

As long as the basic mood and style of the furniture is consistent—formal, informal, country, purist, or eclectic—it is perfectly acceptable, even desirable to mix, though it is always a good idea to get some advice from a professional or a well-trained salesperson/designer when contemplating such a mix.

A really competent store planner will move furniture around for you on the selling floor, so that you can see for yourself how beautifully many of the various American Traditional finishes blend with each other. Most manufacturers of American Traditional furniture produce several different collections from which you can draw.

Furniture arrangement in the dining room, as in the liv-

Dining in an alcove is often expedient when no separate dining room exists. Window seat and dining furniture accomplish this in an area of a large living room.

ing room, must always allow for traffic patterns, so there is no point in trying for a more innovative arrangement if it is not a practical one. There must always be room for family and guests to move around the table, to serve themselves from the buffet, to enter and leave the room.

Many new kinds of furniture styled in American Traditional expressions are now available for dining-room decoration. One is the ubiquitous curio cabinet—also occasionally used in the living room as an accent piece. It has glass sides as well as doors, and is designed primarily for open display of china or collectibles. It is possible to bunch two or more of these curio cabinets together to create an entire curio wall. Most of these designs can be lit from within.

American Traditional dining rooms can also be furnished with the kinds of bookstack, or library, units we described in our chapter on storage. These cabinets usually have concealed storage below, with open shelving or shelves behind glass doors in the upper units. Such cabinets are offered usually in very informal contemporary designs, but they are also available in adaptations of Jacobean, Chippendale, and Queen Anne styles. Some cabinets are even finished off with the flourish of a curved-scroll top.

When bunched together, these library bookshelf cabinets present a long storage wall, and like the curio cabinets offer not only enormous display potential, but also architectural enhancement. Such an arrangement can be very effective in a room that is boxy and sterile, devoid of chair rails or crown or baseboard molding. The cabinets can even turn a corner with the aid of a bookshelf or pilaster corner unit. Slanted open-shelf end cabinets give the arrangement a finished look.

The dining room should always be designed in tandem with any adjacent areas. If it is just off the living room, there should be some consistency in style, and a thread of continuity in the color scheme. Where brown, beige, and red may predominate in the living room, the dining room could be executed in a red-and-white scheme, which would not be an exact duplication of the living-room hues but would in some measure relate to them, and avoid a sudden break in color mood.

Host and hostess chairs are often a popular choice for American Traditional dining rooms; in recent years, many professionals have taken this idea a step further by using nothing but upholstered designs to group around the dining table. The look is different from the conventional approach—quite a bit more luxurious—and best of all, the furniture is much more comfortable. For those families who love to sit around the table with their guests long after a dinner party is over, a set of eight host chairs is a wonderful solution.

Another interesting new look in dining-chair selection is the styling of Queen Anne and Chippendale side and arm chairs in the brightly colored new polyester finishes, which lend the gleam of lacquer but are more durable.

A separate dining room is still preferred by many, but the working mother, as we have suggested earlier, usually prefers the open living/dining/kitchen arrangement, and often will either build or buy a house to contain this architectural feature.

For a while, especially when long and narrow living rooms emerged in new high-rises, people found it necessary to mark off the separate living and dining zones by the so-called "room divider" unit or étagère. These furniture designs were finished on both sides, so that they could be positioned at a right angle to the wall to establish separation of the two areas. In recent years, however, it has been more common simply to let the kind of furniture placed within an area communicate its special use. This eliminates the divider and restores the sense of openness and spaciousness in a large multi-use room.

Building costs may also force a family to buy a house, or rent an apartment, that does not have a separate dining room. In this case, dining usually takes place in an alcove off the living room, in a dining foyer, or even within the living room itself.

Furniture chosen for a dining ell or alcove will, of necessity, be smaller in scale than that chosen for a full dining room. But as we have said earlier, there is much to choose from in American Traditional dining-room furniture that has been specially designed and scaled for these smaller areas—from country rustic to Queen Anne.

Intimate dining for two near
the window of a living room
is established with a small
gateleg table and a pair of
wing chairs.

AMERICAN TRADITIONAL

Dining in the living room can be catered by drop-leaf tables placed against a wall or behind a sofa, or by wall units that contain a table within the base of the cabinet. The table, hidden from sight when not in use, can be pulled out to seat six when the dinner bell rings. For a small family, a permanent game or card table can do double duty for games and dining at different hours of the day.

A large skirted table that sits at the end of a sofa can also be harnessed into dining service when needed. So can an ample writing table, a generously scaled coffee table, or a set of bunching tables or nest of tables. The chair-table, a favorite from early Colonial days, is still a popular style when space is tight and no real dining area exists. Any minor arrangement of the kind described above might prove all that is necessary for someone who lives alone, or for a couple who entertain very informally. There is no cardinal rule that every home must have a standing dining area.

Dining tables themselves are almost always expandable, either because they have drop leaves or flip tops or because they can pull open to receive extra leaves. Many tables are so designed that they store their own leaves. Another way to extend the dining table is with console add-ons that can stand independently against the wall or be bunched together to form one long serving surface. Since these consoles are the same width as the dining table, and in the same design and finish, they can simply be added onto one or both ends when greater table length is desired. This is a wonderful solution for a glass-topped table manufactured with a single sheet of glass.

It is usually a mistake to invest in an expensive dining table for a first, small dining area if you have any expectation of moving into a larger home within a few years. The small table would be out of scale for the new large and separate dining room, and its style might be too formal for use in a family room. The wisest course here would be to buy a dining table of a size, shape, and style that could move with ease into the family room of your next house. Plywood rounds covered with a pretty fabric (possibly matching the

Elegant dining in the grand manner with double-pedestal table and comfortable tufted Queen Anne armchairs, plus long sideboard.

draperies of the dining area or adjacent living room) provide another makeshift arrangement for dining purposes at a low investment. The table base and top, if not the skirt, could certainly be recycled with a new skirt for some room in the next abode.

Choose dining chairs for that small area which could also be moved into a family room, or which are part of a manufacturer's collection that promises to go on for years, and add more chairs when you purchase a longer table.

Occasionally an apartment has neither a dining room, an ell, or enough space in the living room in which to dine. In such instances, the only option may be to create a dining area within the entrance foyer itself. Tables with large drop leaves and a very narrow center are wonderful choices for such halls, because they take up so little floor space. A writing table or console design that extends for seating is still another fine choice for a foyer that serves dinner to the family.

Entrance foyers should be as attractively decorated as possible—more on that in Chapter 15. But it is even more imperative that a foyer which serves for dining be designed with imagination and cachet. A wonderful mural or architectural wallpaper theme will present a vista or view, while a vibrantly colored area rug, or a glamorous smooth floor of ceramic or vinyl tile, will create an animated mood. A bold color scheme will also help out in a small foyer that is sometimes a dining room. So go all out with such background furnishings in any foyer that has to play this double role.

We have concentrated so far on the kind and size and location of your dining area, and the choice and placement of the dining furniture. But our chapter would be far from complete if we did not talk about the other furnishings needed for the room.

There is probably no other room in the house, with the exception of the entrance foyer, where the decorating approach can be so vibrant, so exciting and provocative. Since, as we have already stated, this is not a room for solitary pursuits (unless it also contains a work/study center), you will want to create a festive showcase for your culinary efforts, and a lively stage setting for animated conversation.

If you think that the restrained elegance of American Traditional furniture will prevent you from generating this kind of drama, you are not truly familiar with the extraordinary flexibility of this style genre. The grace and symmetry of these handsome furniture designs will accommodate a striking color scheme, a dazzling wall covering, a jewel-bright area rug to project the sense of splendor and festivity for which you are striving, while also providing the balance of substance and enduring style.

We are not suggesting that you go all out with a psychedelic room design, or a color plan that reverberates; we are simply pointing out that the decoration of the dining room can be far less restrained than that of the living room or bedroom. The reasons are obvious: in addition to establishing a gregarious atmosphere for entertaining, you are decorating a room that is probably used less often (unless it serves other roles) than almost any other room in your house. You will not tire that quickly, therefore, of a more powerful wall-covering pattern or color mix, and you will not require the serenity of mood you might wish to impart to a bedroom, home office, library, or family room.

So indulge your fancy for, say, a sumptuous wall-covering

Windsor-style settee is used in place of two chairs on one side of this dining arrangement.

- Plan your dining room to make it flexible enough to accommodate large formal dinners and buffet suppers or small, intimate parties. It is most important that you create a dining room that suits your lifestyle.

- Work from a focal point and build your room around it. Select your table style and placement first. Keep in mind that there is a variety of styles, finishes, sizes, and shapes of dining furniture.

- Use storage cabinets to add decorative options for display of collectibles or china. Consider some of the modular furniture discussed in Chapter 10 to create corners or entire walls of architectural and aesthetic interest.

- Keep in mind the transition between rooms. The normal passage from living room to dining room to kitchen should be a pleasant and natural one. Create a harmonious link between the rooms.

- Dining rooms can be created out of extra space in any home or apartment. Consider using an alcove off the living room, a foyer or entrance

pattern and drapery treatment, possibly of matching or coordinating fabric that is somewhat fanciful and lavishly trimmed with gimp, fringe, and/or tassels. Let your windows be topped by a beautifully shaped cornice or a sweep of swags and jabots. An area rug might be a carved-look border design in a vibrant color composition, or an exquisitely patterned and colored Oriental. Incidentally, area rugs are preferable to wall-to-wall carpeting in the dining room, because of well-used and narrowly defined traffic patterns and also because of the occasional spilling of food and drink.

Buy that wonderful mirror to hang over the serving cabinet; splurge on a pair of crystal sconces; find one marvelous chandelier, either a fine reproduction or a "steal" at an auction. Collect an assortment of table linens and build up your trousseau of dinnerware so that you can change your table settings as frequently as you change your dinner company. Use your dining table as a blank canvas, in other words, and see how creative you can be in mixing your linens, china, and flatware—designing new looks for dining each time you entertain. Try out fresh ideas for your centerpieces (more on that in Chapter 16).

Those who own a large dining room and use it only for dinner, once a day, or when company comes may wish to get more living use out of the space by converting it into a dual-purpose arrangement. By shifting the dining table off-center, or placing it against a wall, you can allocate enough room for a second activity or area. If the home has no family room, a small sitting or entertaining area could be established here, with a sofa, chairs, and possibly a cabinet or a nearby closet. By utilizing the dining table as a handy work surface for such hobbies, you will be making the room earn its share of the rent or maintenance for your home.

Remember also that while the dining room in today's home may be a shrunken version of the grandiose banquet halls of yesteryear, or may have disappeared entirely from the floor plan, dining itself has spread to other areas of the home. Once relegated almost exclusively to the separate and hall, an area of the living room furnished with pieces that can be converted into dining surfaces.

• Consider creating other uses for your dining room such as a work/study room, hobby center, home office.

formal dining room or breakfast area, dining can and often does take place in the family room (say, when a football game is running overtime), in the bedroom (for weekend breakfasts, afternoon teas, evening snacks), as well as in the living room, where it can be served on the coffee table or a nest of tables in a casual, impromptu manner.

While some Americans may always have dressed for dinner, and still do, there are few homes today where black tie is de rigueur, even for major parties. Most families dine in their daytime clothes; others occasionally supper in their bathrobes. The food that you cook, the way you serve it, and the furnishings you choose for your dining hours are strictly a matter of personal taste and choice.

No other design in the American Traditional idiom can conjure up a greater sense of romance—of luxury, and of the simple, gentle values of a bygone era—than the four-poster canopy bed.

CHAPTER 13
BEDROOMS

A future bride dreams of owning one, a working mother snuggles under its covers at the end of a complicated day, grandparents associate it with fond memories of all the houses and rooms in which they have lived. New reproductions of tester beds are considered by many to be tomorrow's heirlooms, just as the Queen Anne and William & Mary four-posters that survive today are among the most cherished finds of museum curators and private antiques buffs.

Our present approach to the decoration of American Traditional bedrooms is much broader than that of the early colonists, or even those who came later and developed the draped four-poster, or tester, bed as a means of protecting the sleeper from the cold drafts of a New England winter in an unheated house.

The typical seventeenth-century bedroom with its wonderful cross-beamed ceilings usually contained a field bed with an arched canopy frame covered with fishnet lace. Other furniture in the room might include a small chest, a stand to hold a pitcher and basin, a few ladder-back rush-seated or Windsor chairs, a blanket chest, some braided or rag rugs over the wooden floor.

Eventually bedroom design became more luxurious, as colonists prospered and could use more costly fabrics to make full draperies that covered the head wall and came

A feminine bedroom built around a romantic canopy bed.

around the sides of the bed (and were pulled back toward the wall during the daylight hours).

The top-of-the-bed canopy—today straight rather than arched—would be draped in the same fabric as the bed hangings. Sometimes the bed had draperies at all four corners, so that it could easily be enclosed on a chilly night.

A Colonial bedroom might also include a tall Queen Anne–style highboy. In later periods, larger rooms would have space for a desk, possibly a blockfront Goddard design, and one of the comfortable wing or pretty slipper chairs that were often part of the seating group around the hearth. Oriental rugs in sumptuous jewel tones replaced the more humble rag or braided rugs; walls were magnificently paneled or covered in rich damask fabric or flocked wallpaper.

Of course, four-poster beds were not the only designs that evolved for Colonial life. Lovers of American Traditional are all familiar with the cannonball bed—the modified four-poster that does not take a canopy—and the spindle bed, the Shaker hired man's bed, Victorian brass beds, and many other designs.

So a current interpretation of a Colonial bedroom need not be centered around a four-poster, unless there is enough room available for it and you really love and want the style.

Until recently, beds, and for that matter bedroom furniture as a whole, have not been considered top priorities in the decorating scheme of many homes. Up to this last decade or so, the bulk of the decorating money was spent on living-room and dining-room decoration—on the rooms that "showed" when guests arrived. But all that changed as American families felt the crunch of the space shortage and began to preempt their bedrooms for round-the-clock use. Naturally these bedrooms had to be decorated more attractively and more skillfully in order to satisfy the new requirements.

Now bedrooms double as sitting or reading areas, as home study or office centers, as spas for morning exercises, as getaway havens for the parents of the house.

Designing today's American Traditional bedroom, there-

Adaptations of Chippendale furniture designs compose this master bedroom with crewel bedspread, paneled headboard, and Martha Washington armchair.

fore, often entails the planning of a dual- or multipurpose room. As the stereotypical American bedroom was replaced by floor plans and furniture choices geared to the new roles, the more conventional furniture choices and room-arrangement ideas have had to go by the boards.

Still, as we mentioned in our chapter on floor plans, certain basic priorities must be met. A bed for sleeping is the obvious obligatory requirement, and there must also be sufficient storage, as well as adequate lighting for the room as a whole and for bedside reading or any other specific tasks to

Unexpected furniture placement gives this dormer bedroom its unique style; four-poster bed is positioned in the center of the room.

be performed in this room. If there is enough space for a desk, a sitting area, a chaise longue, and so on, these designs can also be added. They can even be introduced into the plan if at first glance there appears to be no room for them—by the method of "strategic substitution." With this approach, a small desk is substituted for a nightstand; a king-size bed is forgone in favor of a queen-size or even smaller bed, so as to make room for a modest sitting area. An armoire will hold a television set and videocassette recorder as well as clothing, so that a morning workout can be practiced to the instruction of a taped exercise program.

Of course, beds also require bedding—the proper box springs, mattresses, and pillows. Since these products are so important to your comfort and health, you should never stint on them. Buy only quality items which the store will stand behind, so that you know they will last. A mattress should be firm, so as to give your back support; always try out the mattress in the store to make sure that the degree of firmness is to your liking. You can purchase a mattress made from urethane or latex foam, but most good mattresses today are made with innersprings for longer life and comfort. Buying bedding is more of a blind proposition, so be sure to purchase it from a reliable retailer who can assure you of construction and durability.

The best way to work out "strategic substitution" in your arrangement for the bedroom is, as always, with a basic floor plan. (Here you may again want to refer to Chapter 8 on room arrangement.) Once you have decided what must be included in the bedroom, draw your templates to scale, cut them out, and see how they work. You can then determine what space will be left over for other designs needed to give your bedroom an additional daytime role or two. It is only by juggling around such cutouts that you will be able to come up with the most balanced and efficient arrangement.

You may discover that you have given the bedroom too many storage designs, and no seating area. A redo of your bedroom closet with a more efficient arrangement of shelves—a more practical partitioning of storage sections; possibly a few built-in cabinets—may preclude the need for so many cabinets in the bedroom itself.

Perhaps the way you have placed the bed has made it take up too much of the room. Wall-hung lamps or even floor lamps can eliminate one or even both of the nightstands that would normally go on either side of the bed. This would make it possible to reposition it against a wall to make space for a much-needed study center; or you might be able to open up needed floor space for your exercise routines.

Remember that nightstands can be small storage chests, not merely tables with a single or double drawer. Beds can also help with your storage problems, especially if they include drawers underneath the bedsprings, as in a trundle bed.

Blue-and-white documentary print is used for skirted table and draperies, on an ottoman, and as hangings for canopy bed in formal period-style interior.

AMERICAN TRADITIONAL

Many of today's manufacturers make the newly popular "bedwall" models in American Traditional design. These consist of two tall chests connected at the top by a shallow shelf which contains recessed lights, and a lower shelf/cabinet against which the bed is set. Some chests are wider than others, but most offer copious storage potential, and many families choose to buy a bedwall as an almost complete bedroom in itself. But think twice before you invest in one of these oversize and overpowering storage walls. It can dwarf a small room, make the space appear lopsided (because all the furniture is on one wall), or impart an undesirable "trendy" look. Many of these designs can be taken apart and rearranged—for instance, the tall chests at either end can be set together to form one large armoire-style design. So if you are buying for such flexibility, make sure that you like the options the design offers. Note, too, that not all of these bedwalls have enough headboard area against which you can prop up pillows for comfortable reading in bed, or watching television.

While the new bedwall, offered in every conceivable style genre, is the conversation piece of the marketplace at the moment, most bedrooms are still furnished with a standard bed, one or two cabinets or dressers, nightstands, and any additional furniture that can be accommodated. Beds vary in size and in kind, including twin or single, full or double, queen and king (the equivalent of two twin beds). You may purchase a complete bed with its own headboard, footboard, and side frames, or select a headboard that attaches to a frame on casters. The frame supports and adjusts to the size of the box spring and mattress.

Storage can be handled by a chest-on-chest and the new double and triple dressers, which didn't exist in Colonial days but are now interpreted in American Traditional styling in order to meet contemporary storage requirements. Highboys are as popular as ever for bedroom storage—but as we suggested earlier, need not be considered purely as a bedroom design; they can easily move into the living room, hallway, or even dining room, if so desired. Conversely, furniture styles that heretofore may have been labeled exclusively as "living room" or "dining room" are finding their way into the bedroom for special storage needs, or simply to provide a change of pace. Such pieces include armoires, étagères, curio cabinets, and modular units, any of which provide superb vertical storage without taking up any more floor space than a chest or a triple dresser.

If you have more possessions than places to put them, see what changes you can make in your furniture plan. Instead of placing a bench at the end of the bed, use a decorative trunk, or even a blanket chest. Or place one of these in some empty space below a windowsill. Oversized baskets can stow under a writing table or next to a comfortable reading chair.

In our preceding chapter on dining rooms, we explained that furniture in the same collection is often displayed together on a store's selling floor so that you, the customer, can see everything available within a specific design and finish. This is also true for bedroom furniture. It does not mean that you have to decorate your bedroom (any more than your dining room) with a matched suite of furniture; you may find it a safe, convenient way to furnish your bedroom, but it is neither original nor personal.

You will be surprised at how many different designs and finishes within the spectrum of American Tradition furniture reproductions blend beautifully with one another to create a far more interesting and personalized effect than that of a bedroom suite. If you are searching for an authentic look, you may want to mix and match very much in the way your forebears did (even though their mixes were usually unavoidable and inevitable, having been acquired or inherited slowly, and from a diversity of sources).

Again, should you wish to add new pieces in your next and, hopefully, larger bedroom, starting with a mix will make it easier to expand gracefully and without disturbing the design integrity of the interior.

Don't overlook painted accent pieces, or even major designs with a painted finish, in planning your mix of styles

The trundle bed, a Colonial mainstay, is a wonderful space-saving design today. Pull-out drawer can hold another bed, linens, or clothing.

and finishes. Some furniture collections are offered in more than one stained finish, and in numerous painted options as well.

The other decorative elements in a bedroom—floor coverings, window treatments, wall coverings, and accents—require different guidelines from those for a dining room or living area.

First of all, the color used for a bedroom should not be too dazzling, too overpowering. "Instant-impact" color schemes may be fine for a dining room or foyer, but not for the repose of a bedroom, even if it is to serve other purposes as well as sleeping.

Serene, subdued, more restful colors should be the order of the day. Again, this is a matter of personal preference—many people enjoy bold and vibrant colors in their bedrooms; but in that case one should take care not to add other jarring notes. If fabric or carpeting colors are bold, then the walls should be either painted or covered in a restrained wallpaper design, rather than anything overscaled or too dramatic. On the other hand, if you are hopelessly enamored of a very lively wallpaper pattern, choose one of its quieter and calmer colors, from the softest hues within the pattern, for woodwork and solid or plain fabrics used elsewhere in the room.

The bedroom is an excellent candidate for a "one pattern" look—the same design applied to walls and used for bedspread and curtains and/or draperies. This approach is especially successful in small spaces or in interiors with oddly shaped and recessed walls, such as those found in top-floor dormer bedrooms. A single wash of pattern blends the walls and furnishings together and achieves a heightened sense of spaciousness, as well as a very charming, cozy effect.

While the same window options are available for the bedroom as for other rooms in the house, it is sensible to choose window dressing that is lighter in feeling and easy to keep clean. Gear the style of the treatment to the shape of your window and the design of the room, making sure you have lined draperies that draw, or room-darkening shades, so that you can sleep, if you wish to, after the sun has risen. Again, for a cohesive look, and a sense of spatial flow, use fabric at the window that matches what is on the bed, and possibly on an upholstered design. This is almost always an effective way to decorate a bedroom.

There is more than one way to dress your bed. Your most popular option is to use ready-made bedspreads, most of which are available with matching ready-made curtains or draperies. Many styles now come in full throws or fitted spreads, though the trend in recent seasons has been to coverlets and dust ruffles. The advantages of this latter treatment are obvious: the dust ruffle permanently covers up the metal frame support, and the coverlet is smaller and therefore much lighter to handle than a full throw or bedspread. Such bed dressing can, of course, be custom-made, but more and more manufacturers of ready-mades are offering greater diversity and more upscale styling and fabrics in their collections.

Another kind of bed decoration that has captured the imagination of both professional and amateur designers in recent years—and for good reason: it's both practical and pretty!—is what we refer to as "unmade bed." This is really not an unmade bed at all, but one whose linens complete its decoration. In other words, the dust ruffle, comforter, sheets, pillow shams, neckrolls and curtains, sometimes even the walls and windows, are all in the same sheet or linen pattern. You have no heavy bedspreads to remove at night or fuss over in the morning. Just straighten the sheets, comforter, and pillows, and the bed is waiting for you to get into at night, merely by turning down the covers! You can even purchase matching towels for your bathroom.

The popularity of this "unmade bed" look has encouraged a proliferation of designer linens, and today you can find just about any pattern, from casual to sophisticated, and any color mix in the once lowly sheet and its coordinates. Best of all, these new linens can add a modern flavor to an American Traditional bedroom without interfering with its overall style mood. The sheet pattern can also be quilted and used to upholster a headboard, or shirred and hung from pole to pole to cover and soften the walls of your bedroom.

Wall-to-wall carpeting, rather than area rugs and carpets, is often the preferred choice for bedrooms. A relatively modern decorating concept, these textures, usually made with new soil-resistant and highly durable synthetic fibers, offer added rewards of comfort underfoot, a warming insulation, and flattering doses of dense luxury. They also provide a sweep of texture and color that reinforces the bedroom's role as *sanctum sanctorum.* Carpet color choices today are especially appealing, as the new synthetics, which take to dyes of various nuances, come through in a startling variety of fresh, clear color expressions and carpet textures. Fully carpeted floors offer the additional benefit of covering up badly marred, defaced, and splintered floors that would be very costly to repair or replace.

For a more authentic look, you can of course top your floors with beautiful Oriental rugs; or if your room is decorated in a country style, then rag rugs or braided or hooked designs would be appropriate. In either case, the wood floors of your bedroom have to be in tip-top condition, or have the pleasing patina of age and wear, for you to use such rugs with impunity.

Creating a focal point, one of the primary challenges of living-room design, is academic in the bedroom. The bed itself is invariably the largest and most commanding furniture design in this room, and becomes thereby its own focal point. This is most pronounced in the case of four-poster beds, with their decorative canopies and draperies, though professional designers have found ways to create visual interest by designing canopy looks even for the simplest of bed designs.

A short canopy effect can easily be installed as a do-it-yourself project. A sheet of plywood, 2 feet wide and as long as the width of the bed, is attached to the ceiling abutting the wall. The underside of the panel is upholstered with a fabric that matches the draperies, bedspread, or bed linens, and a shirred panel of fabric is extended from the ceiling to cover the entire wall behind the headboard. The sides and front of the ceiling panel can then be draped with fabric in pleated folds or ruffles, or, for a more tailored look, with taut edging. The draped fabric extends from ceiling to floor at the side of each panel, and is tied back decoratively to the wall. Any kind of bed can thus be given the extra panache and traditional romance of the canopy look.

In first apartments, or if the budget is still tight, a young couple may be able to afford only a quality box spring and mattress on a frame, and will have to make do for a while without a headboard of any sort. In such cases a little improvisation can go a long way. A wonderful old quilt, the prized first acquisition of a future collection, can hang on the wall in place of a headboard. So can a large framed poster, a small tapestry, or simply a panel covered in the same fabric as the spread or comforter and finished off with a frame of wood or metal. Or, in lieu of any such makeshift headboard, a grand proliferation of bed pillows, neckrolls, accent pillows, and the like can be heaped up at the end of the bed to effect a headboard look. In any event, it's wiser to use such stopgaps than to invest in a cheap headboard that proves neither attractive nor durable.

Creating or establishing dual-purpose areas within a bedroom takes some careful planning, but need not affect the

Lightly scaled adaptations of Queen Anne and Chippendale bedroom designs enhance the spacious quality of this traditional bedroom.

basic look or style mood of the interior. Even the most luxurious and feminine of bedrooms can include a work area, as long as there is room for a desk or writing table and chair. Impromptu dining or late-evening television snacks can take place at this same desk or writing table, or if space permits, at a table that is part of a small but cozy seating group for two, such as a decorative skirted table.

You may also wish to allocate some area of your bedroom to dressing or making up. If there is room enough for a separate dressing table, fine; but a desk or writing table can also serve as a sometime dressing table if you provide it with adequate lighting and can situate it near your closets or storage designs.

If space permits, you can establish a small sitting area with a love seat, one or two chairs, and even a small coffee table. Such a seating arrangement can be an ideal place to serve Sunday breakfast, or to take late suppers in the bedroom. If you plan to watch television in the bedroom, your set should be placed so that it can be viewed from the seat-

SUMMARIES AND POINTERS

- Bedrooms are more lavish and functional today than they were in Colonial days. Moreover, bedrooms are often used for more than sleeping. The modern bedroom often serves as an exercise spa, reading area, or home office as well as a sleeping chamber.

- Storage furniture in the bedroom does not have to be simply a bureau or chest of drawers. By redefining the traditional use and placement of armoires, étagères, curio cabinets, and modular storage units, you can easily incorporate them into the bedroom design scheme and thus enlarge the storage capacity of your bedroom, while adding furniture of aesthetic interest.

- It is wisest when decorating a nursery to use furnishings that can grow as children do, thus eliminating the need to entirely refurbish a baby's room when the children outgrow the stage of infancy. If you decorate with sensible furniture initially, redecorating may involve nothing more than replacing wall and floor coverings. Most important in a

ing arrangement as well as from the bed. Some kind of unit on casters would probably be your best solution.

Many families in small houses or apartments simply do not have any extra space in their living areas in which to enjoy their hobbies. In such cases the materials of a hobby may have to be stored in the bedroom. Here it might be more practical to purchase modular wall storage than conventional bedroom furniture, since such modules offer excellent storage and are often available as corner desk units or pull-out tables—which can be very useful if the hobby involved is sewing, stamp collecting, or any other "clean" activity.

Up to now we have been talking primarily about master bedrooms. There are other bedrooms in most houses, of course, and their decoration will take its cue from the sex and age of their occupants. Little girls' rooms are understandably most feminine, with soft colors and pretty florals, the decorative look carried out in the choice of furniture, window treatment, and wall covering, and reinforced through accessories.

A little boy's room, on the other hand, will be the place for tailored maple beds or trundle styles and for tweed and checked fabrics for a simple window treatment such as a laminated shade or tailored curtains or draperies. Toys, games, sports paraphernalia, and books will be the "accessories" displayed on cabinet tops and shelves, just as dolls and other girlish collectibles will be the most predominant accents in a girl's room.

A word about nursery furniture. Avoid the Mother Goose school of decorating, with its tiny-tot furniture covered with nursery-rhyme decals. The most practical way to decorate a baby's room is to choose furniture that will grow up with the child, so that a change in floor coverings, window treatments, or wallpaper will be all that may be needed to help the room graduate from one stage of childhood to another. Also, contrary to a formerly popular notion, young children, even babies, love bold primary hues. So choosing the once obligatory baby blue, pink, or yellow for a nursery is not child's room is the play area, which can also house modular storage furniture that you can add to through the years as the need for storage grows.

- Floors and walls should be treated differently in the bedroom than in the living room. Colors should not be too dazzling; it is better to opt for subtle and soothing color schemes in the room in which you rest and sleep. If you do prefer bold colors, then you can add balance with wall treatments: use either subdued paint or restrained wallpaper designs. Also ideal for bedrooms is the monochromatic color scheme, which can blend walls and furnishings together to open up the space and create a cozy atmosphere.

- Many people prefer wall-to-wall carpeting for the bedroom; the luxury of soft, warm carpet is ideal for comfort and insulation.

only limiting, it may even be less preferable to the baby.

Light-blocking shades, ample storage potential, and some kind of comfortable play area are essential for a child's room. And the older a child is, the more he usually owns. That's why it's wise to invest initially in open-stock modular storage furniture, perhaps in any one of the many Shaker-inspired designs now on the market. You can then add more modules as the child matures. A teenager may want his own computer, television set, and stereo, and you will need ample shelf and table surface to house these electronics. Reasonably priced computer desks are part of the current explosion of electronic storage furniture, so check these out if your teenagers are computer-literate.

Since many parents of grown children prefer to stay in their empty nests, rather than move to a smaller house in a new neighborhood, or retire to a condominium community, the rooms that once housed their children are often converted to guest rooms. Or a guest room may already exist in a house large enough for its lively family to enjoy the luxury of a spare room.

Guest rooms should be furnished for comfort, adequate lighting, and sufficient storage. Huge cabinets or dressers are hardly necessary, since guests usually stay for a short time and most guest rooms have limited wall space. If there is space, choose twin beds rather than a double one, as this is the more generally preferred choice; those sharing a bed at home will not mind splitting up at your house, while those used to separate twin beds may not sleep well if forced to make do with one bed.

If your guest room doubles as a home office, study area, or other center of activity, some kind of convertible bedding such as a dual-purpose sleep sofa or daybed would be preferable. Manufacturers are now making new versions of the old Murphy bed, hiding them in handsome cabinetry. Remember, any time you place a dual-purpose sleep design in a room, to be sure that any coffee table you use with it is light in weight, so as to be easily removed when the bed is pulled out or down.

AMERICAN TRADITIONAL

The term "family room" was officially born in the middle of this century, although the role of the family room—as an informal, relaxed, and convivial family center—harks back, as does

CHAPTER 14
FAMILY ROOMS

that of the dining room, to those warm and cozy keeping rooms of Colonial days.

When the family room did emerge on the American scene, it came in a pervasive manner. The time was the 1950s, the era of the great building boom following upon the heels of World War II. Starved for new living space after the strifeful war years, when residential construction had virtually come to a halt, Americans responded with fervor to tract houses which they could purchase with government loans and which contained this newly conceived and labeled living space.

It was the era of "togetherness," as magazines extolled the return to closer family unity, to shared pursuits and leisure time. This was the new goal for families whose roots had been all but destroyed when fathers and husbands donned soldiers' uniforms and left to go overseas.

The family room, as it evolved during this period (for a while it was known as the "great room," when in many houses the family room replaced the living room and was conceived, along with the kitchen and dining area, to function as a single living totality), was a carefree center of family enjoyment, a place where two or more members could congregate, watch that other postwar innovation—television—and not worry about "messing up the house." Furniture was informal, fabrics were in only the most practical

Navajo-inspired print, dark pine furniture, and rich earth tones augment the Southwestern style of this small family sitting area.

L-shaped arrangement of color-
fully striped sectional sofas provides this animated family room
with its major seating.

textures and colors, floors could be mopped clean or were topped with rugs or textured carpets that concealed stains and traffic marks. When company came, the family room served as an adjunct to the dining room and living room for buffet entertaining, and for dinners or suppers based on the newly popular "casserole cookery."

Adjacent to the kitchen as well as to the outdoors, and usually accessible to a patio or terrace through its sliding glass doors (another postwar architectural invention), the family room, when in tandem with backyard space, served as the site for a new kind of summertime entertaining: the cookout. The sudden proliferation of charcoal grills all around the country demonstrated the popularity of the new outdoor broiling and roasting obsession—a relaxed, easy way for suburban Americans to entertain or to cook weekend dinners.

Today the family room is still an important part of the American living scene, whether as a component of the original architectural plan, a space added onto the house, or simply a transformation of one room into another. An extra downstairs bedroom, an underused dining room, a newly enclosed breezeway all can provide family-room living. So too can a living room that has been converted from formal parlor to mellow living space, simply through well-designed redecoration.

Now, with the coming of the electronic revolution, we are more likely to hear "media room" or "entertainment room" as the term for this informal living area. While still serving a multiplicity of roles, this born-again family/media/entertainment room is now more and more the place that holds and organizes our burgeoning collection of electronic equipment.

You may wish to ask at this point: how does this new entertainment room, filled with space-age electronics, relate to the subject of American Traditional decorating? The answers are both simple and several.

First of all, the decoration of this media room can easily be executed in traditional style: with furniture designs in informal country finishes, rough textures, and easy-care rag or braided rugs. Secondly, the kind of wall storage, now being referred to as "electronic furniture," that is needed to house this equipment is today available in every furniture design expression, including formal and casual American Traditional, Country French, elegant English, and sleek contemporary interpretations.

Dual-purpose family room in a condominium contains both a seating group and a dining/game-table arrangement.

If you need a large entertainment cabinet, or a complete wall system that will provide enough storage for component stereophonic and television equipment, you will find a wide choice in the marketplace, with many such units containing pull-out swivel shelves for the television set or monitor. Other space-conserving designs include storage modules or vertical cabinets that move easily on casters, so that they can be placed in different areas of the room as needed.

So the family/media/entertainment room continues as a popular living space in the American home of the '80s—and for other reasons than the new living requirements of the electronic age.

Families today, whatever their electronic inclinations, have considerable need of ancillary living areas in their homes or apartments, especially if the living room is an elegant or sophisticatedly decorated space. This extra living area is all but critical for a family with older children or with two adult generations—parents with teenagers or college students, or families whose postcollege children still live at home or for economic reasons have temporarily returned. Obviously each set, older and younger, will need a separate place to entertain friends, turn up the stereo to eardrum-breaking volume, and so on. An auxiliary, carefree, and separate family room makes this possible.

And there is still another factor: in today's servantless world, entertaining buffet style—even if based on the currently popular nouvelle cuisine, rather than the starchy casseroles of the '50s—demands as much seating space as possible. The family room can be brought into play as an extra area in which to place guests for such through-the-house affairs, or for other special occasions such as children's birthday parties, Super Bowl suppers—in fact, any kind of large celebration.

In addition, with more leisure time than ever at our disposal, we need a special place in which to indulge a hobby and store its diverse and often excessive equipment. A family room can accomplish this for us with wall systems that include open and concealed storage, copious shelf space, desk units, pull-out tables, even specifically designed modules that transform one area of a family room into an instant sewing center or home office. (A word of caution here: do not go out and buy such a wall system to house a "sometime" hobby, one you are likely to drop next year for something entirely different. The storage requirements for one hobby or another can be vastly different.)

All these activities—entertaining, the pursuit of hobbies, the enjoyment of the most up-to-date audio and video equipment—demand some kind of informal living center that contains durable furniture (the kind you can put your feet on), wear- and stain-resistant fabrics and floor coverings, and a casual mood that encourages us to truly enjoy our relaxed and stress-free moments.

Decorating the family room should take its cue from the kind and number of roles the room is to play, the furniture required to satisfy these needs, and the overall style mood preferred.

This last determination is the easiest. Since the room must provide a comfortable and casual atmosphere for all its activities, the style of the furniture must be relaxed. Here is one interior you are most likely to furnish with rustic pine, oak, and maple designs in the American Traditional mode. Sofa and upholstered chairs should also be in a casual style. A wing sofa is a popular choice for a family room, if the American Traditional look is to be emphasized. Other styles, such as a comfortable and informally covered Lawson-style, will also do nicely. A configuration of seating modules in contemporary design will update the mood of the room; in traditional styling, available in many of today's upholstered collections, such modules can also be a fine choice for family-room comfort. Fabrics can run the gamut from houndstooth checks and American plaids to contemporary country textures—any of which will work into the casual feeling of the room, and can be purchased in weaves that have the protection of a stainproof finish.

Another furniture design that often serves a multiple role in the family room is the standing game table, which can be

Two-story family room with
comfortable upholstery centered
around the brick hearth contains
home office facilities in desk
placed behind one of the sofas.

When no family room exists, add one on. This greenhouse addition was transformed into a dazzling sitting space with matching sofa and love seats all in green to blend with the trees and shrubs.

used for informal dining as well as for poker, bridge, puzzles, and other games. Consider adding such a piece if space allows, and if your family could make good use of such a setup.

With graph paper and templates in hand, you can start to juggle the floor plan of your family room—checking all the while how much wall space is available to accommodate the kind of storage system you hope to buy. You should also be evaluating whatever free wall area remains after allowing for the furniture necessary to house all your electronics and hobby paraphernalia, provide desk or work-surface facilities, and offer adequate shelf area. If most of the available wall space is to be preempted by storage units, you may, of necessity, have to place your seating designs out in the middle of the room. Be sure, when you plan this, that the seating will comfortably face the television set or any other fixed projection screen. Also, if you plan to do a great deal of informal dining in this room and find you do not have the space for a permanent game-table arrangement, try to make space either for a large coffee table or for a nest of tables that can be opened up when needed.

Assuming you and your family will spend a lot of time in this family room, it is advisable to compose a color plan based primarily upon serene neutrals, or soft, easy-to-take tones with possibly a few bright accents. Avoid a mix of brilliant hues, or an "instant impact" color scheme that hits you between the eyes before you can turn on the television set. Any excessively animated color scheme can be tiring and at odds with the low-key mood of comfort and ease for which you are striving.

The site, size, and specific use of the family room or area should give direction and discipline to its decoration. Many of the new and more compact houses, or some of the wonderful reclaimed and remodeled barns, feature a dramatic two-story living and dining space, with small bedrooms constructed from whatever extra footage remains on the first and second floors. These houses not only are popular choices for leisure or vacation homes but, as studies have recently noted, prove the ideal size for a career couple, retirees, or a one-child family.

In such houses, the living space *is* the family room, so the decorating approach should cater to the needs of both kinds of rooms. Arrange for ample seating by providing a comfortable conversation group. Also attempt to include as much cabinet and open-shelf storage space as possible; this might mean the inclusion of a storage wall. Other methods of enhancing storage potential would be to substitute small chests or cabinets for the usual end tables, or include decorative chests or baskets that could fit into a small wall space or under a console table; or add a hutch or other kinds of storage furniture as space permits.

The seating furniture could be grouped around the focal point of a fireplace, while also positioned for comfortable television viewing. Since the dining area is often part of an open living-dining floor plan, the dining table could be utilized as well for hobbies, games, or even the pursuit of handcrafts. In that case, you should probably choose a dining table that can expand, when needed, to serve at a dinner party, but still be large enough as it stands to serve its other desirable purposes. Chairs should offer firm back support, when part of this dining group, and can be pulled into the major seating arrangement when the occasion requires.

Remember too that your living/family room (as well as a separate family room) will often double as a guest room. The sofa, therefore, should be a dual-purpose sleep design. If you hope to use a pair of sofas, you'll find many designs in both convertible and stationary versions.

Traffic lanes should be carefully plotted, so that they do not interfere with the flow of conversation or the enjoyment of music and television. If there is not enough room for a hobby that requires privacy, you might want to relocate space for such a pursuit in one of the bedrooms.

Something more stylized—not quite as casual or rustic as the style of a separate family area—might be preferred in a living room that doubles as a family room. You can certainly orchestrate such a more formal atmosphere as long as you are careful to choose stain-resistant fabrics, easy-care floor coverings, and furniture impervious to frequent use. The relaxed, convivial mood of a multipurpose area can still be provided in a living room with the kind of style you prefer. Even if such a room does not work out to be quite as imposing as you might have wished, what you gain in terms of family use and enjoyment makes the trade-off more than worthwhile.

An attractive family room without a sofa; instead, an oversized chaise and several comfortable seating designs.

Many houses, especially older ones, were not designed to include a separate family room—a circumstance that can become an increasing liability as a family grows and living needs accelerate. But rather than requiring a move to a bigger, more expensive new house, the problem can often be solved through remodeling with an add-on room. This is

SUMMARIES AND POINTERS

- Family rooms are leisure rooms, hobby rooms, entertainment rooms; they are, in other words, multipurpose informal gathering rooms and as such should be decorated to accommodate the many different functions they serve for the family.

- Comfortable and casual furniture with multiple storage units often sets the stage for the basic design.

- Traffic lanes in the family room should be carefully thought out and planned so as to allow for multiple, concurrent activities. Arrange the room as though there were several rooms in one. This will create specific areas for activity and expand the potential of the room.

especially easy to accomplish if the house has ready-made areas to fill in (such as a single-story screened porch or an unused breezeway, attic, garage, or basement). Some of these spaces will need refacing and additional insulation in the course of new walls, paneling, and flooring, and an attic may need a skylight. Garages also require the installation of new walls, windows, ceilings, and floor, and all remodeled areas need new and often built-in lighting as well as sufficient heating and insulation.

Replacing screens with new walls, windows, floor, and proper lighting will transform a no longer fashionable breezeway into a comfortably sized family room that has the advantage of first-floor location and proximity to living and cooking areas.

In any remodeling project, you should seek the advice of professionals and get estimates up front, and from more than one contractor. It can also pay in the long run to hire an architect, or an interior designer with architectural expertise, to work out the plan and advise you on the kind of walls, soundproofing, flooring, doors, windows, and other construction materials best suited to your particular project. Whether your room is on grade or below grade will direct your choice of flooring and other materials.

The abiding American country look is a wonderful choice for these kinds of remodeled areas. It also works beautifully in an extra bedroom turned family center, or in a remodeling project where a wall has to be removed so that two small areas become one spacious interior. What we are suggesting here is that you return to the mood of the Colonial keeping room with its barn siding, rough-hewn beams, large hearth, painted hutches, random planked flooring, provincial prints, American collectibles, and rag rugs. Once the room or rooms have been architecturally converted, this ingratiating country decorating approach can take the project to its most rewarding conclusion.

The family room has become an almost indispensable adjunct to contemporary American life. The higher costs of gasoline and of eating out have once again made the American home the center of entertaining that it was in the 1950s, but with an important difference. Now large-screen television, cable stations, videocassette recorders, home television movies, and radical innovations in audio—such as the digital disk and Beta or VHS high-fidelity (television with stereophonic sound)—have secured this new family/media/entertainment room as the wave of both present and future.

With the proliferation of home entertainment equipment and the heightened interest in cooling and nutrition among all members of a family, it is easier and less costly to stay and entertain at home. It is also more fun. Thus the family center will continue to serve the American home in its broader and continually expanding role.

First impressions count—a fact that many of the earlier Americans obviously appreciated much more than some of us who tend to treat our entrance halls in a perfunctory manner. A wall-

CHAPTER 15
ENTRANCE HALLS AND FOYERS

paper is chosen, some carpeting put down, perhaps a table and bench or chair added, but often there is no real planning, no carefully considered design scheme that will transform the entrance hall into the inviting, cohesive, often dazzling area it deserves to be!

Not so with our colonists. They understood the importance of a gracious welcome. Their greeting to entering guests started, in fact, at the front door. Often the door was quite elaborate, especially in the more prosperous postrevolutionary periods, when the houses themselves were more substantial and luxurious. Fanlights, leaded windows on top and sides, and beautiful paneling distinguished these fine doors, as did doorknobs or latches and all the wonderful ubiquitous Colonial knockers with which the visitor announced his arrival.

Eighteenth-century American entrance halls were inordinately handsome, even when simply and sometimes sparsely furnished. Graceful, often dramatically shaped balustrades and staircases dominated these foyers and introduced the grand flourish of an imposing architectural element. Balustrades turned, or were winding and circular; occasionally double staircases led from the front hall up to the first landing. Railings and treads were fashioned from richly grained

Stenciled border, deacon's bench, and grandfather clock lend a gracious American Traditional flavor to this entrance hall of a contemporary house.

woods; the sides of the staircases were often embellished with carved motifs set below the treads. The newel, or downstairs front end, of the railing might be shaped in a fanciful baroque spiral.

The entrance hall in larger houses was exceptionally spacious, often large enough to contain an ample seating arrangement almost comparable to what one might expect to find in a small or even good-sized living room. But even if the size of the foyer was limited, other attributes enhanced the area. In many homes, the entrance ran the full depth of the house, so that upon entering the front door you could gain a view of the rear garden, should the back door be open or paned with glass.

Magnificent paneling, usually painted, also graced these entries, and incorporated built-in niches or recessed cupboards crowned by delicate shell motifs. The open shelves of these niches often displayed a priceless personal collection of imported porcelains.

Scenic hand-blocked wallpapers gave the walls of Colonial foyers a dramatic cachet, and also a feeling of space and luxury. In the later and more resplendent houses of the truly affluent, marble floors were installed in dramatic black-and-white diagonal checkerboard patterns. In most foyers, however, floors were of highly polished wood, and topped with the jeweled effect of small Oriental rugs. Often three or more of these rugs were needed to cover enough of the floor, especially if the hall led from front to back door.

Exquisite furnishings completed the design of these striking spaces—imposing grandfather clocks; handsome console tables and cabinets; chairs, settees, and sofas of the period, as well as decorative mirrors, chandeliers, and other accessories. All in all, Colonial entrance halls were remarkably beautiful and gracious, a fitting introduction to all the wonderful rooms that lay beyond.

For these same reasons of proper welcome and introduction to your home, as well as to meet other contemporary requirements, it is even more important today to give your entrance hall a sense of grace and space, the enhancement of

A minuscule foyer is given a sense of drama with oversized painting and mirrored pedestals decorated with plants and accessories.

When space is limited, only one piece of furniture may be accommodated, as in this handsome Windsor settee in a tiny entry.

AMERICAN TRADITIONAL

beautiful furnishings, and an integrated interior design.

Because an entrance hall or foyer in a contemporary house or apartment is more often than not of modest size, certainly much smaller than the entries of elegant Georgian houses, one can afford to splurge on the furnishings themselves. This might be the place to give in to your passion for a very spectacular and expensive wall covering, since not many rolls will be needed. One or two small Oriental rugs of fine quality will not be nearly as costly as those needed for a larger area. With only enough room for a chair and table or cabinet, buy the very best you can afford to augment the aura and charm of the area. An entrance hall is not the spot for hand-me-downs or remnants of a former house or apartment that have no other place to go in your new home. But on the other hand, you should not go so grand that your entrance hall will be out of sync with the rest of your home.

The foyer or entrance area should always connect or relate to surrounding spaces, possibly a living room on one side and a dining room on the other. The color schemes of these adjacent areas can be different variations on the same theme, but a common thread of colors should tie them together, however loosely. The major color in the entrance hall could be a minor accent in the living room, while a dominant hue in the dining room could reiterate one of the less important colors chosen for the foyer. In this way all three areas are linked together, even though each retains a separate identity.

Entrance halls are not merely pretty areas to look at or in which to greet entering visitors; they also serve certain functions. Here is where overshoes or boots may be put on or taken off, so that some kind of chair or bench will be necessary. A table to receive unsorted family mail just removed from the post box, or a surface where one can put down small packages, is also essential. This surface could be the top of a small chest containing enough drawer or cabinet space to hold gloves, scarves, knitted hats, extra sweaters, and any other items that the family wants to have handy in the front hall.

A good-sized mirror adds sparkle and a feeling of greater space than actually exists in a small foyer; it is also a practical adjunct to any entry. Here the family and guests can adjust their hat, overcoat, and scarf, or simply make sure that their hair looks right and their makeup is fresh.

An entrance hall in a small apartment often has to double as a dining area. If this is the case, then a drop-leaf, gateleg, or flip-top table would replace the more usual console. A chair would be placed on either side of the table, with additional matching chairs to be brought in from the living room. Folding chairs or stackables, stored in a closet, can also expand the use of a foyer/dining area.

It is important, especially if your entrance has to serve this additional role, that you provide adequate lighting. This can be in the form of a chandelier or ceiling fixture that may run the gamut from a humble Colonial design in hammered or pierced tin to shimmering brass to even the most splendid of chandeliers dripping in crystal. Additional lights could also be offered by a pair of sconces straddling a painting or a mirror. Built-in ceiling spots or downlights will enhance the general lighting of an area, particularly if the room is windowless. Spots can also be directed on a cherished painting or antique to dramatize the object and make it more visible. All lighting elements should be put on dimmers for a wider range of nuances.

Other ways of coping with the windowless aspect of an entry are also rewarding. Take a cue from the colonists and use a scenic wallpaper to construct a beautiful "view" in a *trompe-l'oeil* effect of space and spaciousness. An oversized mirror, or an entire wall paved with mirror, will also multiply the feeling of space and the optical illusions it generates. If the foyer is used frequently for dining, make sure that the floor decoration is a practical one. Treat a wood floor to several coats of a protective polyurethane finish. Rugs that can be sent to the cleaner's are preferable to the permanently installed wall-to-wall textures. Brick, set in a herringbone design, will emulate the floors of early Colonial houses; it is

New wallpaper and paint restore the long foyer and staircase of this
18th-century house. Blockfront chest in foreground holds gloves,
scarves, and sweaters, provides a place for mail and small packages.

also practical and can be the basis for a wonderful indoor-
outdoor garden approach. Black-and-white vinyl tile is an inexpensive way to copy the checkerboard marble floors of yesteryear.

For stair treatment, a word to the practical: buy durable
carpeting in a color and texture that will not show the dirt.

ENTRANCE HALLS AND FOYERS   279

SUMMARIES AND POINTERS

- **The foyer is a room and should be designed as such. Moreover, it is the welcoming statement to your entire home or apartment. When decorating an entranceway, treat it as a gracious space and give it the elegance and beauty of furnishings and accents it deserves.**

- **Keep in mind that the foyer is a transitional space, a passageway to other rooms in your home. Though the color schemes and decorating motifs can differ from foyer to living and dining rooms, there should be some unifying element of color or pattern. This will create harmony and grace.**

- **Entranceways are also functional spaces, where one leaves messy shoes and wet umbrellas; as such, they should contain a chair or other small seating unit, a table, and any other storage furnishings needed for use by your family and guests.**

Low-looped pile, densely woven and in a texture that resists skidding, is usually desirable. The stairs can be completely carpeted (in which case they are called "upholstered"), or else a narrow width can be tacked down as a runner with the exposed wood part of the stairs given a long-wearing, nonskid finish. All stair carpeting should be padded, even if it is only a runner; so should small accent rugs on the entrance-hall floor, to prevent falling or skidding.

Of all the rooms we have treated, the dining room lent itself most readily to our sense of invention and playfulness, to our need to indulge a whim for a trendy color scheme, or to the capricious selection of a superdazzling wall covering. This is also true of the entrance hall. Here we can decorate with more abandon. Here we can go all out with a modish fabric pattern or an elaborate chandelier. We do not live in our foyers, so we will not tire of them quickly. Bold colors used here will not distract us from our more solitary pursuits or hobbies, or keep us awake at night. And since we want our entries to be inviting and sparkling, why not use the space to do something different, even a bit *outré?*

Turn the walls of your hall into a minor art gallery; find one fabulous porcelain umbrella stand; hand-stencil the risers of your staircase; mirror an entire wall; amass a collection of European posters; use an unusually bold and unexpected color for background, possibly in a shiny enamel finish; invest in a sensational wallpaper, or blanket the walls with an overflowing collection of botanical prints.

Other indulgences come to mind. An antique William & Mary console table, which might be lost in your large living room, will have a place of honor when it is the only piece of furniture in a small foyer. If you can find a shallow Welsh dresser or stripped-pine hutch, you might wish to place it here and display your impressive assortment of redware. If there is space enough only for a slip-seated chair, cover it in that fabulous flame-stitch weave; it may cost an arm and a leg per yard, but you'll need so little of it.

One supersized, eye-stopping painting can change a ho-hum foyer into a place of enchantment. So can a marvelous fabric print used to skirt a round table placed in the center of the space.

A final word of caution: don't crowd your foyer. Use only as much furniture as it can gracefully accept, for it is better to underfurnish than to overfurnish an entry. With so much attention given to walls, floors, and decorative accents, not as much furniture is needed visually.

An American poet once said that you should pack your boat of life with "only what you need—a home and simple pleasures." These simple pleasures could easily be construed as those loving touches

CHAPTER 16
ACCESSORIES

and slowly collected accents that make a home so warm, so personal and inviting, so very much a "one of a kind."

Perhaps you have already succeeded in furnishing your rooms with just the right choices of furniture, fabrics, and floor coverings, allocated and positioned in what appear to be workable as well as attractive arrangements. Your colors blend in a way that pleases the eye and soothes the psyche; your window treatments are superb elements within a cohesive architectural and interior design structure. But it can all still fall apart unless the accessories and accents you choose complete your rooms from the standpoints of function and visual effect. Accomplishing this will make them warm, ingratiating, and memorable.

Many of us know some person who went out and tried to "accessorize" in a single day. Such an effort almost surely ends up looking slapdash or automatic—the fruit of a frantic, almost robotlike procedure.

For collecting accessories—finding just the right answers for the top of your living-room coffee table, the dresser in your master bedroom, the hutch in your dining room, the walls of your library—takes hours and hours of "treasure hunting." A silver tankard, a wooden butter mold, a primitive painting, an amber vase, or a worn but still beautiful Oriental rug—these may all be designs that happen to strike your eye at an auction, at a flea market, or as a reproduction

Attractive placement and juxtaposition of magazines, candlesticks, and wood and ceramic accents distinguish this unusual coffee table in charming coordination with wall accessories.

283

A magnificent collection of porcelains is symmetrically arranged on the marble top of a 19th-century cabinet.

at your favorite department, furniture, or gift store. You buy things you fall in love with at first sight, then find a place for them. You don't fill in the empty holes as quickly as you can.

There are, of course, some helpful guidelines to the choice and placement of accessories, but it is always better to leave some areas empty than to run out and purchase an accent just so you can feel your home is complete. For accessories offer a rare opportunity: the chance to express yourself in a way that couldn't be done with the other purchases you make for your home.

While such factors as budget, function, space, and architectural parameters may have limited your freedom of choice in the selection of furniture fabrics or floor coverings, you can more easily indulge a fancy or a whim, even an obsession, when you choose your accessories and collectibles. Some of these may serve more than an aesthetic role—practical objects such as lamps, pillows, ashtrays, baskets, trunks—and others will be merely decorative. Any and all of them should be chosen essentially because they please you and your family and will enrich your home.

If you are using a professional to help you decorate your home, you can still handle the accessory part yourself, perhaps with a few guidelines from your designer. Not only will this give you the opportunity to make your home more closely express your own personality and that of your family, it will also soften and humanize that "perfectly decorated" look which sometimes results from a professional job.

If, on the other hand, you are decorating your home yourself, you will certainly want to carry the plan through to the final stages. Even if your home is furnished temporarily with some hand-me-downs or expedient furniture pieces, don't abdicate the task of finding some wonderful finishing touches. They may be just what is necessary to pull it all together for the moment.

WHAT ARE ACCESSORIES?

Accessories is a term that includes many different kinds of decorative accents—lamps, paintings, prints, and collectibles. An accessory is almost anything that is not a piece of furniture, a rug or carpet, a wall covering, or fabric. This covers a lot of territory.

Accessories include anything that hangs on the walls—paintings, sconces, clocks, barometers, signs, tapestries, old tools—as well as accents for tabletops, cabinet shelf surfaces, open shelving, and the tops of dressers, chests, cabinets, desks. There are hard accents, such as pewter vases, wooden boxes, porcelain or ceramic plates, crystal pitchers, stoneware crocks, and so on. Soft accessories, which usually decorate different areas than do hard accents, incorporate the whole range of fabric accents, from pillows and quilts to shawls and afghans. And as already mentioned, there are accessories that are functional as well as decorative—such as lamps, wastebaskets, ashtrays, and candlesticks.

There should be some consistency in your choice of accessories, though there is also room for digression. If you want to give an eighteenth-century-style interior a somewhat more contemporary personality, you could introduce a modern canvas, some sleek crystal vases, or other elements that will combine with your period-design furniture for an eclectic and possibly more interesting result. Certainly it will be more personal!

As you collect accessories, you should be buying regardless of what is trendy and in fashion at the time. Don't rush out to buy an Art Deco lamp just because it's "in" at the moment. *Do* buy it if you like it and will continue to enjoy it after the fad has passed.

You will discover in the process of shopping that you not only are choosing things that you like but already have some rough ideas as to where they will be put. "What a perfect painting for over the mantel!" you'll say. Conversely, of course, you may purchase a piece unexpectedly, and then somehow manage to find just the right spot for it in your home. This is possible as long as you haven't already passed the limit, with not another square inch available. For whether you prefer the Spartan purity of an underdecorated home or the colorful clutter of an abundance of furnishings and accents, sooner or later you will have reached the point where you must stop—unless yours is one of those families who can afford to go overboard and buy more paintings and accessories than they have room for, keeping the surplus in the attic or a spare closet, and juggling accessories around when the spirit moves them.

The style of each room, the number of table surfaces, and

Blue-and-white traditional collectibles give period flavor to a modern fireplace shelf.

the amount of wall space available will give you some direction as to the number of accessories you need and the areas to receive them. Remember, however, that this is a dynamic and fluid process. A box you might first have chosen for a hall console could ultimately find a place on the living-room coffee table, especially if you find something much more appropriate for the console. If you have planned from the start to use such accents as pillows, paintings, quilts, and lamp bases or shades to introduce spots of bright color into a neutral scheme, you will use this approach as a guideline when you purchase accessories and wall decoration.

Accessories can be employed most successfully to dramatize the specific mood of a room. Exquisite porcelains and silver accents will augment the formality of a Chippendale living room, the sumptuousness of a Sheraton dining room. On the other hand, folk-art collectibles, hand-wrought pot-

in blown, cut, pressed, hobnail, and other kinds of glass textures, most of them available in a magnificent array of colors.

Mantel, shelf, banjo, and grandfather clocks were the outstanding shapes that emerged with the beginning of clockmaking in this country, while lamps of cast iron, brass, and wood; tin wall sconces; and Paul Revere lanterns were among those lighting designs which are still collector's items, even in this age of electricity. So are the brass and crystal candelabra that are now often electrified so that they can be used in today's rooms, or are reproduced in marvelous copies of the period originals.

The litany of American accessories or collectibles goes on and on. To name a few: stoneware jars, jugs, crocks, and pitchers; brown-glazed Rockingham ware produced in Bennington, Vermont; the elegant bowls, pitchers, porringers, teapots, tankards, and plates developed by New England silversmiths; decorated tin- and toleware in the shapes of pitchers, trays, canisters, lidded bowls, teapots, and coffeepots; old carpenter's tools and antique flatirons. Also noteworthy is our extraordinary heritage of primitive paintings; butter and cookie molds made from oak, maple, or walnut; wrought-iron trivets in an endless variety of designs; folk-art toys, slipware, redware, and spongeware; baskets, black dolls, Shaker boxes, ironstone, graniteware, scrimshaw. We could go on, but this will give you some idea of the scope; there are many reference books on American accessories for a fuller grasp of their diversity.

TABLETOPS

Some refer to the decoration of a coffee table, end table, or even a bedroom dresser top as a "tablescape." What is really meant by this is that accessories are not just placed randomly on a table but are arranged in some kind of ordered fashion. A coffee table may hold a set of art books, a large plate (for an ashtray), a plant, a box, a piece of sculpture.

You can use a minimalist approach throughout your home and be assured of keeping your table surfaces relatively uncluttered. And if you stick to it as a deliberate choice, the sparseness of accessories will enhance the sleek look of your rooms, rather than make them seem unfinished.

On the other hand, if the look you desire is one filled with details and *objets d'art,* you must give a great deal of consideration not only to what you buy, but also to where you put your choices. Since the coffee table is part of a conversation group, one of the focal points in any room, be sure to arrange its elements so that the composition is a relatively strong one. Avoid using small and "ditsy" items, especially if the coffee table is low and large, in which case you should also leave enough room to accommodate a coffee tray, a platter of hors d'oeuvre, or some glasses, for entertaining needs.

The best way to start your tablescape is to put down the essentials first—such as a lamp, an ashtray, or even a tea service (if that is where you wish to keep it at all times). Then build up around the essentials, adding whatever you have collected that will work in terms of space, shape, balance, height, and texture. Remember to juxtapose objects of different shapes, heights, and sizes for balance and eye appeal.

Night tables also need certain essentials, such as a telephone, radio, ashtray, but depending on the size of the table you can add any number of optionals here—small boxes, picture frames, books, even a limited number of collectibles.

Desks require certain priority accessories, such as a blotter, a container for pens and pencils, possibly some reference or address books, even a box of stationery. Beyond this, you can add other items, such as picture frames, some silver-topped or porcelain jars for paper clips, a decorated box to hold letters to be answered, and so on. Even if you can work with only the basic items because space is limited, you can still arrange these pieces artfully, not just place them willy-nilly on the desk top.

Your bedroom dresser may also require such fundamentals as a lamp, perfume tray, brushes, possibly a decorative box to hold assortables, some picture frames, a small mirror.

A simple but charming composition of accents enhances the surface of a classic pine dresser in a master bedroom.

Here too you can augment where possible. If your dresser is long enough, you might find space for a collection of glass bottles, small Shaker boxes, some folk-art pieces.

Use juxtaposition whenever you arrange a tabletop. Put down the elements to be used in an interesting manner, so that they relate in such a way as to create a pleasing and memorable composition. Use thought, skill, and finesse. Try moving your items around on the table until you arrive at the most visually effective result, close up and from a distance. It can happen suddenly: after paying your dues with trial and error, it all clicks and you realize you have finally "gotten the hang of it."

The uninitiated may ask: how do I start buying my accessories? One way is to go through books and magazines and get some input on how the professionals do it—what they select and how they arrange their groupings. But don't follow their example in a copycat fashion. Let their ideas trigger inspirations of your own. Try also to recognize what may be strictly faddish—an effect simply for the sake of being dramatic. Designers will do this from time to time.

The kinds of tabletop accents available are more numerous than can be covered here, but certain basic categories are worth mentioning, not only because they are attractive and versatile, but also because they often serve a secondary and functional role. Baskets, bowls, boxes, candlesticks, decorative plates, and stacks of books and magazines are common choices. The first three items can hold plants, fruits, flowers, and such cocktail helpers as coasters and napkins. Candlesticks add needed height to a coffee-table arrangement and can be lit for romantic illumination.

You may have considered the almost obligatory stack of magazines or books to be a coffee-table cliché, but such stacks do add a strong shape to the tabletop design, and provide guests with something to look at while you are mixing drinks or putting the final touches on dinner.

Another understandably popular cliché is the cluster of picture frames on a single night table, end table, or even a large skirted table in the bedroom or living room. If you love to show off your family and friends, then go for the picture-frame tablescape, cliché or not.

In grouping collectibles, mix wood with crystal, ceramic, iron, basketry, enamel, brass, silver, tin, pewter, and so on. The more materials you blend, the more provocative your composition will be.

Or try a different tack, assembling elements that share a commonality of texture or color. You could combine disparate designs in the same color family (different shades or tints of blue, for instance), or all natural textures (driftwood, rocks, shells, straw baskets), or simply the same style (American Traditional, formal or country).

Try to be daring occasionally; it usually works. A large sculpture, an oversized box, a weathervane on a stand, a giant painted wood watermelon slice can give enormous panache to tabletop arrangements. Group a pair within some sparkling hurricane globes.

DINING-TABLE TOPS

Even those who put enormous effort into arranging the tops of their coffee and end tables, their nightstands and dressers sometimes overlook the table surface which gives them the greatest opportunity to be creative, to make their meals memorable, to constantly change the "canvas": the dining table.

It is not enough to put some dried flowers in a bowl and set down the arrangement as a permanent centerpiece, trotting out the same tablecloth, napkins, flatware, and china each time you entertain. Just by exercising a little imagination, you can generate fresh excitement with the same basic wardrobe of table elements, and compose an arresting table landscape that changes from one occasion to another.

Instead of dried or fresh (and probably too expensive) flowers, use a clutch of potted plants or flowers for an ongoing centerpiece, for when the table is not set. When company comes, try out some new ideas gathered from other areas of your home. You could borrow a mix of small sculptures from the living room, say, or collect assorted candlesticks sitting around on mantels and end tables. Bring in small folk-art pieces, removed temporarily from a hutch. Or create your own candlesticks, using large apples or artichokes as bases. Or simply adhere your candles to some decorative plates.

Use a dining occasion to show off the newest additions to your collections of small spongeware pitchers or wooden decoys—a few in the center of your table.

Mix the colors of your napkins and place mats so that they do not match; experiment with new ways to fold napkins; buy some colorful or decorative napkin rings. Borrow a quilt from the end of the sofa and on occasion use it as a tablecloth. Try out new and interesting ways to set a table buffet style—blend country baskets with elegant china, or mix stoneware serving bowls with narrow crystal vases filled with different flowers of the same hue.

WALL DECORATION

In contemporary decoration, the latest approach has been to use one large painting, rather than the once very popular wall collection. This can also work for American Traditional rooms, unless you intend to establish a look of country clutter. In that case you will probably want to use your walls to hang many of your collectibles, such as baskets, molds, a collection of pewter plates, redware, heart-shaped tinware, even cooking utensils. Primitive paintings, old documents, and botanical prints and samplers might also be worked into such arrangements.

Contemporary wall hangings could be used if you want to give your home a more eclectic style. Collections of mirrors, posters, fans, screens, small contemporary rugs, even exotic articles of clothing such as jackets or hats can prove unexpected and very effective elements in a wall composition.

You could also consider using an oversized mirror or a large quilt over a cabinet or sofa, instead of the more usual single and outsized contemporary canvas. The look will be just as dramatic, yet fit more naturally into your American Traditional interior.

A word of caution about hanging. A single painting should be easily viewable at eye level, no higher and no lower. The same applies to groupings. You can first try out such a grouping on the floor. Juggle the elements around until you have arrived at what appears to be the most provocative solution. And keep in mind that accessories are not supposed to fade into the wall.

SOFT ACCENTS—QUILTS, AFGHANS, PILLOWS, SHAWLS

As you have probably surmised by now, hard furniture pieces such as tables, dressers, and cabinets get hard accents of porcelain, pewter, and brass, to name a few possibilities, while sofas, love seats, beds, and chairs are embellished by the warming and brightening touches of pillows, quilts, afghans, and other soft accessories.

Pillows are not only decorative: they are virtually indispensable. Many new sofa designs, in fact, have loose pillows in a bunch of sizes rather than tight backs. Pillows pamper a sofa and make it warm and inviting, not to mention more comfortable.

SUMMARIES AND POINTERS

- Unlike furniture, accessories offer you an opportunity to express yourself in whimsical, unique ways. An accessory may be a lamp, painting, print, or collectible—in other words, anything that is not furniture, rug or carpet, wall covering or fabric. To put it still another way, an accessory is anything that hangs on a wall or rests on a tabletop, open shelving, or a desk, cabinet, sofa, or chair.

- When selecting the kinds of accessories for your accenting, you must also determine placement. Keep in mind that there should be some theme, some consistency to your collection as well.

- Balance and symmetry are the most important considerations in decorating with accessories.

- There is considerably more decorative freedom these days with regard to wall hangings. You can group fans, mirrors, posters, or small contemporary rugs, or hang a quilt over a cabinet or sofa instead of the customary large canvas. Remember, however, that a single painting should be hung at eye level, as should groupings.

Pillows come in large, small, and medium sizes. They can be bought ready-made in almost any style, shape, or color you could wish for, or you could have them inexpensively custom-made, perhaps from the same fabric you are using for draperies or the sofa.

For a while, the new round-edged "Turkish" pillows, with no welts, were a fad with designers. Now it seems that knife-edged pillows are back in favor. Ignore these trends if you wish, and buy whatever you like and whatever you think will go best with your upholstered pieces and other elements of your rooms.

Sizes can also be trendy—one year tiny pillows are "in"; the next season, huge, oversized styles are all the rage. Select the size and shape of pillow that best complements your chair or sofa and adds the needed comfort for your back, as well as a welcome spot of color and pattern for the room.

The larger soft accessories—quilts, afghans, and shawls—can be added or done without. The choice is a personal one, again to support whatever mood or look you wish to achieve. These expansive soft touches can add rich tactile nuances to the back of a sofa or, when folded, to the foot of a bed. Quilts introduce the kind of pattern and color that may be absolutely necessary in a room filled with few or no fabric motifs. Shawls and afghans inject interesting textures and weaves; they are also handy to have around in chilly rooms, or for when the oil burner is on the fritz. These accents give interiors a human dimension; they immediately convey the message that someone lives there, however fixed and formal the room's decoration.

A special word should be added here about how and where to dramatize with quilts. Use a brightly colored one on the wall of a room with pale or off-white hues. An old quilt with damaged corners can make a round table skirt. Add several quilts to your bedroom—as a coverlet, on a blanket stand, folded for display on the open shelves of a hutch. If you are an obsessive collector of quilts, you can change them around—adapting the Oriental fashion of rotating flowers with the four seasons—to give your rooms a different look every so often. A certain number of quilts will be kept "in stock" on an open shelf, the rest spread around your home.

Every house has a certain amount of existing space for displaying accessories and collectibles—recessed niches, built-in bookcases, beams and soffits. Usually these prove insufficient, especially for an addict of American memorabilia. In our chapters on storage, living rooms, and dining rooms, we covered many of the different kinds of furniture that can organize, house, and display your collectibles. In addition to the time-honored hutches and china cabinets, there are now available, in the American Traditional design expression, many such storage designs as library bookstack units, curio cabinets, and étagères, as well as modular storage systems that contain copious open shelving as well as concealed cabinet storage.

We have referred earlier in this chapter to the many kinds of American collectibles that might convert you into a hopelessly obsessive habitué of flea markets, auctions, antiques shops and shows, or beaches (for shells and driftwood). If that is or becomes your fate, you had better think seriously about sufficient and appropriate space to display all your old treasures, on-hand and anticipated. To give them greater impact, you should group collections by kind and put them in the same hutch, in one pair of étagères, placed next to each other on a single wall, or on one oversized coffee table. Don't mix them up; they won't be nearly as fascinating to your guests or as satisfying to yourself.

Of course there is a point when enough is enough. Don't let collectibles take over your house. If you can't add more built-in shelving, you may have to put your collecting to a temporary halt. That, or move to larger quarters.

Collecting is rewarding and enjoyable. It satisfies a deep urge to possess things, it links us with the past and with earlier generations, and it gives our rooms and our furnishings a very personal character.

Throughout this book we have celebrated the versatility and flexibility of the American Traditional decorating style. We have stated time and again that it lends itself not only to a purist expression,

CHAPTER 17

AMERICAN TRADITIONAL IDEAS FOR CONTEMPORARY MAGIC

but to adaptations that range all the way from a minor up-dating with fabrics and colors to those freewheeling eclectic mixes that are as contemporary in style and spirit as any room furnished exclusively with modern elements.

In this final chapter we will show you some of these wonderfully dramatic, fresh, enterprising, disarming, exuberant, and crisp contemporary looks that can be expressed with American Traditional furniture.

One example illustrated on these pages is a solar house built in New England and decorated in the American Traditional style. The living room has white walls and a white sofa and carpet, but delicious hothouse colors in fabrics and in the one huge modern canvas. The oak table in the dining area is surrounded by four armchairs and two host chairs, all in American design and all covered with the same large-scale

Crimson enameled walls, white upholstery, bordered area rug, and chinoiserie cabinet create decorating excitement in this elegant sitting room.

Contemporary and traditional American furnishings are
mixed for a vibrant solar-house living area decorated in yellows, whites, and terra cottas.

The surprise of seeing American country furniture and antiques in a New York City loft is what gives this large living space its special decorating magic.

Not what you would expect to find in a ski-vacation house: American Traditional furniture, with one large armoire of Country French inspiration.

fabric check. Modern paintings on the walls and the dramatic contemporary architecture of the two-story space give it great verve. Vibrant colors and modern accessories also lend excitement to the bedroom. The result: a memorable modern house that just happens to be furnished with American Traditional.

Would you ever expect a modern loft in the factory district of New York City to be filled with antique American country furniture and collectibles? You may not have thought of it yourself, but one innovative designer did just that. We show this loft next. It is all dressed up for a Christmas evening; the open space is very much a part of contemporary urban life, but all the furnishings are indeed collector's pieces from the past.

An A-frame ski house has the drama of a two-story living room and the warmth and comfort of American Traditional furnishings. We include it here as another example of how decorating magic can derive from the unpredictable and unexpected use of this furniture style. Had the ski house been furnished with modern designs, it might have been just another vacation house. Very often the use of American Traditional in a modern setting produces an effect more visually exciting and vibrant than if it were given a contemporary treatment.

Two furniture groupings, both angled out from the walls; a delicious color scheme of mauve, pink, and white; and the glitter of mirror and glass add up to a dazzling living-dining room.

American Traditional and Country French enter the electronic age in a media-room design for the enjoyment of music and television.

Other examples follow, and indeed abound back through the pages of this book. An all-white living room (except for one red chair) totally avoids the stereotype, yet the major seating pieces and tables are of Queen Anne design. Another living room derives its grand cachet from red-lacquered walls, white sofas, and an area carpet of deep blue bordered in stark white.

Lively patterns and colors can also make a difference, as demonstrated by one living room with glowing peach walls, sofas in a blue-green–and–peach floral print, and floors topped with accent rugs whose motifs coordinate with the colors and patterns of the fabric.

Executing the "unmade bed" (see Chapter 13) lends high vitality to a reproduction of a paneled Jacobean four-poster bed in a room filled with Chippendale and Queen Anne adaptations. The colors of the linens are orange-red and yellow, and these hues are carried through in the carpeting and some of the accessories. The room faces a lushly planted atrium, the perfect adjunct for a home in the Southwest (which it is).

Nothing could be more up-to-date, you would expect, than a home designed for a woman television producer on the move. Yet here again, American Traditional shines. The angled placement of the living-room furniture, the jewel tones and lush textures of pink and cranberry velvets add up to a superbly efficient modern American living space. Best of all, the den (or second bedroom) has been designed around an entertainment center that organizes television and stereophonic equipment. There is also room for a projection screen.

American Traditional furniture has stepped into the electronic age, and its future remains certain and secure. For three hundred years it has been an important part of our history, of our heritage of decorative arts. Its dominance will continue just as long as Americans cherish and respect its superb hallmarks, and find fresh, enterprising, masterly new ways in which to use them.

GLOSSARY

AFGHAN: woolen shawl or coverlet, knitted or crocheted, or composed of crocheted squares sewn together.

APOTHECARY CHEST: chest with many small drawers (or simulated ones), adapted from Early American druggist's chests.

APRON: structural part of table or chair, placed at right angles to underside for increased support and decorative trim.

ARMOIRE: inspired by the tall, often beautifully carved furniture closets of French design, today's versions come in any style expression, are often fitted inside to serve as a bar or store electronic entertainment equipment.

AUBUSSON: flat-woven handmade French rug, originally woven on the looms of Aubusson; often hung on a wall as a tapestry.

BACHELOR'S CHEST: small-scale chest of drawers.

BATWING HARDWARE: brass hardware used on cabinet doors and drawers and resembling the shape of a bat with its wings spread.

BERBER: rug of undyed off-white wool yarn, made in a flat weave in a horizontal ribbed effect, or sometimes with a plaid or simple woven design.

BONNET TOP: name for the tops of highboys, secretaries, or headboards that feature a broken scroll pediment at the center.

BROKEN PEDIMENT: also known as scroll or bonnet top, this eighteenth-century embellishment was an outgrowth of the flat-topped designs of the previous century. The bonnet rise is broken in the center and often finished with a scroll motif on either side, while an urn, carved miniature bust, or other such ornament is centered between the two scrolls.

BUN FEET: ball-shaped feet or terminals seen on late-seventeenth- and early-eighteenth-century cabinets.

BUNK BED: two beds or bunks, structured so that one is directly over the other, much the way bunks are fashioned for soldiers' barracks

or small staterooms on ships. Top bunk is reached by a ladder.

BUTTERFLY TABLE: table with rounded drop leaves that are supported by brackets shaped in the form of a butterfly's wing.

CABRIOLE LEG: leg with a pronounced curve to its knee.

CAMEL-BACK: one of the first sofas, a Chippendale design, its back rising or curving like a camel's hump.

CANDLESTAND: small tripod, pedestal, or four-legged table, used to hold candles and their drippings.

CANNONBALL BED: bed with a large ball capping each of its four low posts.

CANOPY BED: tester, or tall four-poster, bed with fabric canopy, often with bed draperies (originally designed to ward off drafts) as well.

CAPTAIN'S CHAIR: armchair with a saddle seat and low curved back with vertical spindles.

CHEST-ON-CHEST: two-sectioned chest; the one mounted on top is usually smaller.

CHEVAL MIRROR: adjustable mirror that swings between posts. Small versions, often with drawers in base, are used on chests or tables.

CHINOISERIE: painted furniture whose delicate motifs are executed in the colors and designs of Chinese furniture embellishment.

COBBLER'S BENCH: once a shoemaker's work seat with drawer for tools, it is sometimes adapted as a coffee or occasional table.

COMB-BACK: style of Windsor chair whose spindles resemble an old-fashioned high comb.

COMFORTER: another term for a bed quilt.

COMMODE: originally an enclosed bedroom "chamber box," later combined with a washstand. Now the term means a nightstand or console chest.

CONSOLE TABLE: table usually without drawers and taller and longer than an occasional table; used in hallways or as a serving surface in a dining room. Some console tables can be widened by the extension of leaves.

CORNICE: can be either a projecting molding on the top edge of a piece of furniture or the decorative wood structure that reaches across the top of a window to cover hardware. Either painted or upholstered.

CREDENZA: tall storage cabinet, usually made with doors rather than drawers.

CURVED STILES: the undulating shape of the outside wood frame of a chair, such as that of the Queen Anne splat-back design.

CYMA CURVE: the shape of the front and side stretchers of the low frame of a William & Mary chest or other designs. The curve swells toward the back of the design rather than toward the front.

DENTIL (MOLDING): decoration for cabinets (also walls and built-in cupboards) of small rectangular blocks set under the projecting cornice like a row of teeth.

DHURRIE: flat-woven wool rug made in India, distinguished by its geometric interpretations of a variety of motifs. Colors are usually soft, but bolder looks are now also available.

DISTRESSED: the finish of a new furniture piece, usually a reproduction, which has been so marked, nicked, and blemished that it simulates the patina, or "hand," of a well-worn antique.

DOUGHBOX: deep, slope-sided box, once used for raising bread dough, adapted for occasional-table design with a roomy storage compartment.

DRUM TABLE: round lamp table with deep apron, sometimes revolving on a pedestal base, whose shape resembles a drum.

DRY SINK: the original took water for washing dishes; today's version is a cupboard with an open well on the top, often lined with a copper tray to be used as a bar or to hold plants.

DUST RUFFLE: decorative skirt, with a flat center expanse to cover the box spring, which hangs in folds to the floor to conceal the metal frame of a bed.

DUXBURY CHAIR: another term for Windsor chair.

ÉTAGÈRE: tall storage design with open shelves set in tiers. Some designs have cabinet space at the bottom.

FAN-BACK: fan shape characterizes the back of this version of the popular Windsor chair.

FIDDLE-BACK: chair whose splat back is shaped in the form of a violin.

FLUTING: vertical channels carved into columns or pilasters, as first seen in ancient Greek architecture.

FOLIATED SCROLL CARVING: incised designs on early Jacobean chests that combined scroll and foliage motifs.

FRETWORK: open and interlacing geometric woodwork design, used to ornament furniture or to make a decorative screen.

FRONT STRETCHER: support connecting the two front legs of a chair.

GALLERY: decorative railing around the edge of a table, shelf, or tray.

GATELEG TABLE: William & Mary style with two drop leaves and legs that swing out like a gate to support them.

GIMP: another term for welt, cord, or narrow tube of fabric used to cover tacks that hold upholstery fabric to frame of chair or sofa, or added merely for decoration on furniture and window treatments.

GRILLE: the grillwork design of metal or wood used to reinforce glass cabinet doors.

HARVEST TABLE: very long table with narrow drop leaves that run the entire length. Originally used for feeding harvest hands.

HIGHBOY: tall chest of drawers, usually on cabriole legs with bonnet or broken-pediment top (eighteenth-century design). Earlier highboys had flat tops and straight legs.

HITCHCOCK CHAIR: named for early Connecticut chair maker. Derives from a Sheraton design called "fancy chair," and usually has an oval top rail. Often painted and decorated with stencils.

HOOP-BACK: another variation, also called "bow-back," of the popular Windsor chair, named for the rounded hoop or bow shape of its back.

HUTCH: storage design with open shelves above a base containing cupboards and/or drawers.

JACQUARD: fabric with woven rather than printed design. Early Colonial looms created popular geometric, floral, and documentary jacquards.

JAPANNING: decorative technique that seventeenth-century English cabinetmakers, influenced by magnificently lacquered Oriental furniture, introduced of applying many coats of paint and varnish to furniture so that the motifs were "raised"; occasionally gilt was added.

JOGS: protruding wall beams or structural supports.

KILIM: flat-woven rugs with geometric and floral motifs, distinguished by rich and dark colors; first made in the Middle East, now manufactured everywhere thanks to their popularity for both traditional and contemporary interiors.

LADDER BACK: refers to the runged effect of a chair back that has many horizontal slats.

LAMBREQUIN: decorative window frame, usually made of wood and either painted or fabric-covered. Similar to cornice, but frame extends down the sides as well as across the top of the window.

LAWSON: low-backed chair or sofa design in which arms are often set back to accommodate a T-shaped seat cushion.

LAZY SUSAN: round, revolving tray sometimes used for the center of dining and coffee tables.

LOUVERS: shutterlike slats—movable on window shutters, fixed when used for decorative door panels on cabinets.

MAJOLICA: style of colorful, enamel-coated decorative pottery which originated in the fifteenth century.

MATE'S CHAIR: smaller than a captain's chair and with shorter arms.

MISSION: furniture style, very simple in shape and decoration, that is typical of designs used in the Spanish missions of the early American Southwest.

MULLIONS: slender vertical and horizontal bars or molding that divide the glass panes of doors and windows. Colonial windows were multimullioned, as glass could then be made only in limited sizes.

MURPHY BED: traditionally, a bed stored in a wall or closet; now may be concealed behind cabinet doors in a tall storage piece such as a contemporary armoire.

NECKROLL: small, cylindrical bed pillow, feminine and decorative, that can be used to support the neck from behind.

OGEE FOOT: foot support for cabinets, shaped like a bracket with a double curve.

OTTOMAN: armless and backless low seating design, often completely upholstered and made with a skirt.

PARSONS STYLE: shape of a table or sofa leg based on the T-square, evolved by the Parsons School of Design in New York City.

PEDESTAL: center support for a tabletop, which may have a single foot or can have a tripod base. Extension dining tables often require two pedestals for firmer support of the top.

PEMBROKE: small rectangular table with two drop leaves, shallow drawer.

PIERCED SPLAT: openwork, or "pierced," treatment of center splats of Chippendale chairs, in contrast to the solid splats of the Queen Anne style.

PILASTER: grooved or fluted columnlike embellishment, often added to cabinets of classic design.

PILLOW SHAM: pillow cover with flanged edges that protrude beyond the pillow for a pretty and decorative look.

REDWARE: collectible American pottery so named because of its red color; it was made from the same clay used for making bricks.

REVEAL: the paneled or unsheathed recess that runs from an inside wall to the outside window. Reveals were deep in early Colonial houses because of the thickness of the outside walls.

ROCKINGHAM WARE: cream-colored pottery, spattered with a brown glaze, first made in Bennington, Vermont, in the nineteenth century.

SADDLE SEAT: seat scooped away, for greater comfort, to sides and back of a chair from central ridge, which resembles the pommel of a saddle.

SATINWOOD: decoratively figured pale yellow-gold hardwood, favored for highly polished early-nineteenth-century furniture designs.

SAVONNERIE: elaborately designed, high-pile hand-woven rug, first made in France in the eighteenth century, in softly colored floral and scroll motifs.

SCRIMSHAW: whalebone that has been incised with designs, a craft that American sailors once used to busy themselves on long voyages.

SECRETARY: tall and slender desk with drawers below and open or closed bookshelf unit above.

SETTLE: high-backed all-wood bench, often of Windsor design, with arm at either end; sometimes called a deacon's bench.

SHIRRED FABRIC: fabric gathered on a pole so that it hangs in tight folds. When applied to walls, the fabric is shirred on two removable poles—one set high on the wall, the other close to the floor.

SHIELD-BACK: chair design, introduced by Hepplewhite, whose back is shaped like an open shield or heart.

SHOJI: Japanese-style paneling made of translucent rice paper and wood frames, used in Japan as sliding partitions and in American homes as wall and window panels or for simple yet decorative screens.

SISAL: strong tropical fiber used for making rope, recently popular as an inexpensive floor covering.

SPINDLE BED: bed with decorative turnings, like some chair backs.

SPLAT BACK: the center section of a chair back, such as the solid splat of a Queen Anne chair or the pierced (open) splat of a Chippendale design.

SPONGEWARE: mottled pottery on which color has been applied with a sponge, then glaze added before firing.

SPOON FOOT: simple, flattish end of a cabriole or turned leg.

STENCILING: motifs applied to furniture, walls, floors by means of cut-out patterns, so that the paint color penetrates only through the openings of the design. Results in a more

disciplined motif than freehand painting, and is one that can be exactly repeated.

STEP TABLE: originally made to reach high bookshelves. Adapted today, with the steps kept to two or three levels, designs can double as end tables.

STRETCHER: support connecting and bracing legs or lower frame of any piece of furniture. Stretchers are frequently turned or shaped for decorative interest.

STRIPPED PINE: pale finish of pine country furniture, from which all added stain has been stripped away to reveal the natural graining and color.

SWAGS AND JABOTS: popular eighteenth-century window treatment in which a length of fabric is swagged and hung at upper corners of a window by rings or decorative hardware. The fabric descending at the sides of the window forms the jabots.

TAMBOUR: narrow strips of wood mounted on fabric, such as that used to cover a rolltop desk or for the movable door of a cabinet.

TAVERN TABLE: very long table constructed of wide boards, usually of pine.

TRESTLE TABLE: long, rectangular table with vertical support at either end connected by a deep stretcher. This trestle replaces the usual legs or center pedestal as the table support.

TRUMPET LEGS: cabinet and table legs on early William & Mary furniture, so called because they simulated the shape of a trumpet.

TRUNDLE BED: low bed on rollers which fits under a single bed. Can also pull out like a drawer from the bottom of a single bed.

TURKISH PILLOWS: soft-contoured, unwelted pillows with rounded edges.

WAINSCOT OR PANELED CHAIR: design with a solid wood back similar to paneling used for walls or wainscoting.

WINDSOR CHAIR: characterized by slender turned spindles, wooden saddle seat, and splayed, turned, or raked legs, joined by stretchers. A very popular style, expressed in numerous variations.

WING CHAIR: upholstered chair with high curved sidepieces, or wings, originally contrived to ward off drafts.

INDEX